EAST
OF THE
ODER

Meiner gütigen Mutter mit den klugen Augen.
To my loving mother with eyes full of wisdom.

EAST OF THE ODER

A German Childhood under the Nazis and Soviets

LUISE URBAN

'One day, early in February, I went outside to play in the yard. I had a little boy with me who was about six years old, he was the son of refugees staying with us. We were bombarding a tree with snowballs to see who could achieve the most hits. It was fun. A Russian soldier appeared in the driveway leading to our yard and took pot shots at us. Little Richard fell down in the snow, dead … I walked back into the house and said, "They have shot little Richard".'

The author and publishers would like to thank Clare Agnew for all her help in the creation of this book.

First published 2013 by Spellmount,
and imprint of The History Press
The Mill, Brimscombe Port
Stroud, Gloucestershire, GL5 2QG
www.thehistorypress.co.uk

British Library Cataloguing in Publication Data.
A catalogue record for this book is available from the British Library.

ISBN 978 0 7524 9103 5

Typesetting and origination by The History Press
Printed in Great Britain

CONTENTS

INTRODUCTION

It is not necessary to understand the military and political background to this story. As Luise Urban says herself, she has not delved into the historical record or attempted to verify facts. She has simply set down her own childhood memories of a horribly cruel period in history. Her experience, the sufferings of her own family and the torment of all those civilians (not to exclude the soldiers and POWs) east of the Oder are described with a terrible clarity. Some readers, however, may find these brief notes of use. Why, for example, is the Oder the defining border of misery? Why did the Russians treat *Polish* POWs and refugees with such appalling brutality?

Before the Second World War, Germany's eastern border with Poland had been fixed at the Treaty of Versailles in 1919. Certain adjustments were made to the line to allow for the ethnic composition of small areas beyond the traditional provincial borders. Inevitably, some people were left, or felt they had been left, on 'the wrong side of the line'. Upper Silesia and Pomeralia (eastern Pomerania) were divided, leaving areas populated by Poles as well as other Slavic minorities on the German side and Germans on the Polish side. A further complication was that the border cut Germany in two: the so-called Polish Corridor and the 'Free City' of Danzig, established to provide Poland with access to the Baltic Sea, were populated predominantly by Germans. History shows that when lines are drawn on a map and nations or countries are not 'naturally' defined over time by geographical features such as mountain ranges or rivers, tension or disaster often follows, from the Balkans to the Indian subcontinent, from Iraq to several modern African states such as Nigeria, where ethnic enmities led to the tragedy of the short-lived state of Biafra.

The Oder–Neisse line (*Oder-Neiße-Grenze*) is the German–Polish border drawn in the aftermath of the Second World War. The line primarily follows the Oder and Neisse rivers to the Baltic Sea west of the city of Stettin. Hence Winston Churchill's memorable and prophetic judgement of 5 May 1946: 'From Stettin in the Baltic to Trieste in the Adriatic, an iron curtain has descended across the Continent.' All pre-war German territory east of the line and within the 1937 German boundaries was discussed at the Potsdam Conference (July–August 1945). Germany was to lose 25% of her territory under the agreement. Crucially, some might say (including most certainly Luise Urban) callously, the 'Big Three'– Stalin, Churchill and Truman – also agreed to the expulsion of the German population beyond the new eastern borders. This meant that almost all of the native German population was killed, fled or was driven out. The Oder–Neisse line would divide the German Democratic Republic (East Germany) and Poland from 1950 to 1990. East Germany confirmed the border with Poland in 1950. West Germany only officially accepted it in 1970. In 1990 the reunified Germany signed a treaty with Poland recognising it as their border.

The Third Reich's last battle is usually identified as that for Berlin, a doomed last effort with the Führer directing it from his bunker.

INTRODUCTION

It can be argued, however, that the last concerted battle was actually directed by *Generaloberst* Gotthard Heinrici. He took command of Army Group Vistula (*Heeresgruppe Weichsel*) on 20 March 1945, before the enormous Soviet thrust towards Berlin was launched in April. Heinrici, not Hitler, decided that there was only one strategic course left for Germany: to hold the Soviets back along the Oder Front long enough for the western Allies to cross the Elbe River. The war was lost and Heinrici accepted it. All that was left was to bring the western Allies as far as possible east to save as many as possible of the German population from the fearsome revenge that would overtake them at the hands of the Soviets. Defending the Oder Front might force General Eisenhower to order his armies into the planned postwar Soviet Zone of Occupation, as outlined in the top secret western Allies' plan, *Eclipse*, which was designed to prevent the Soviets from 'overstepping the mark' westward – into Denmark specifically – and gaining the access to the Atlantic she offered. Berlin, Heinrici ordered, would not be defended. OKW (*Oberkommando der Wehrmacht,* Supreme Command of the Armed Forces) decided on 23 April to defend the capital. This left Heinrici at odds with OKW over operations along the Oder Front. His defence against the Soviets was undermined. On 28 April, Field Marshal Wilhelm Keitel discovered troops under Heinrici's command marching away from Berlin against the Führer's orders. A furious Keitel tracked down Heinrici and accused him of treason and cowardice. Heinrici was relieved of his command the next day, as an endless procession of wounded and disarmed soldiers and refugees streamed past, fleeing from the Soviets.

This summary of events in 1945 east of the Oder tends to construct an inadequate or misleading 'net' of cause and effect to throw over the chaos that led to the deaths of millions of innocent people, including most members of Luise Urban's family.

FOREWORD

I am living far away from the place of my birth and home to me is now a place where I have been asked constantly: 'What are you doing here? Where do you come from?' So, I will tell my story. Not because I think I am a gifted writer and the world should know about it. No, but because it is only reasonable to explain to my children where I come from and why I am here.

This is the story of my childhood. Sadly, it is not suitable to be read by children.

I am German, but have written this in English. To recall the past in German is far too painful and I could not, remotely, tolerate it. In addition, my extensive knowledge of German vocabulary and therefore better choice of words would make it impossible for me to pass on accurately the trauma I suffered as a child. To relive past events in English is the distancing mechanism I need to recount my early life. Writing in English means I can safely sit in a glasshouse and look out, or rather back, as what I am about to relate cannot hurt me any more. There is a barrier between me and the world I am describing. That world is crystal clear and I can give an almost detached account of it. It is with great sorrow that I must insist I am writing about events that truly took place.

You may throw as many stones as you like at my glasshouse. It will not break. I am indestructible.

THE WRONG SIDE OF A RIVER

I was born on the wrong side of a river at the wrong time in history. The times I am writing about are the Hitler years and the immediate post-war years. It was a tragic time for the world and I had the misfortune of being born on the eastern side of that big river, the Oder.

My family was well-to-do with a sizeable property and a large house, which could not only accommodate four generations of one family but also one of my uncles with his family and a separate flat for a very kind, very old lady who had helped to bring up my father. When he got married she wished to live in his house so that she could be with her little Johnny.

I know little about the wide-ranging backgrounds of close members of my family, as all records were destroyed during the war. Out of 26 of us who lived in the house, only 9 survived 1945; and then there was no one left to ask. I know that my maternal grandfather was the descendant of an Italian rebel who had to flee Italy after the Garibaldi uprising. He settled somewhere in Slovakia and my grandfather stems from that lineage. He spoke German and Slavonic, which was his first language. He was a very stern, principled man with a keen interest in astronomy and the humanities and he was one of the few people that I know who could recite Goethe's *Faust* from beginning to end by heart.

My great-grandfather on my mother's side was very special too. His rooms were full of books and beautiful china, which he collected. When the day's work was done, he used to read and read and read. He had a lovable weakness: he adored cooking for me, his eldest great-grandchild. Needless to say, I was happy to hang around in his rooms for the glorious food, with books and newspapers stacked high on the table.

No one taught me to read but with my great-grandfather reading aloud to me at times from newspapers I was able to make sense of the large, printed squiggles. It was hard though, because the print was the highly ornamental old gothic German print. But I cracked it without help. No one in my family took any notice of my ability to read at a very young age; apparently everyone in my immediate family could read long before school age. It was accepted as normal. Breathing, eating, drinking, reading – that's what children did.

Sometimes my great-grandfather would speak to me in a strange language; it probably sounded like Dutch. He was actually descended from Dutch dam builders whom Frederick the Great had attracted to live and work in Prussia. They were expert dam builders and the Oder needed damming up with extensive earthworks, up to 30m thick in places. They lasted until they were destroyed in 1945. As a result of many years of neglect thereafter there were catastrophic consequences for the area.

I much later discovered that the language in which my great-grandfather spoke to me was not really Dutch but resembled closely the old Gothic, which was classed as a dead language no longer spoken and understood. It had clearly travelled from the south down the Rhine, pockets had survived and then, under Frederick the Great, it had come to the east of the Oder with the dam builders.

I had as a grown-up no difficulties reading the *Hildebrand*, the *Hildebrandslied* Saga in Old High German. The language diversity in my family was accentuated by my great-grandfather's wife, great-grandmama Gauthier. She was from French aristocratic stock. Her family survived Bartholomaeus Night (the Saint Bartholomew's Day Massacre of 1572). During the night of 23/24 August many leaders of the French protestants – Huguenots – were assassinated, apparently on the orders of the Queen Mother, Catherine de' Medici, and many more Protestants were murdered by the mob. Great-grandmama's family escaped and fled to Prussia. Their descendants lived under the protection of Frederick the Great. Most of them settled in Berlin, but my great-grandmother followed her husband to a town east of the Oder and as a token of her love for him accepted German nationality to honour him, the first and only one from all her family to do so. Great-grandmama was a most beautiful woman. In their part of the house you would hear French; in my grandparents' part you would hear Slavonic. But we all spoke German in public. In the 1930s and 1940s it would have been most unwise to utter foreign sounds, which could have fatal consequences.

I know little about my father's family, except that they had suffered greatly in the First World War. Two brothers had gone down in U-boats and when my father was five years old his father was crushed by a heavy piece of machinery that had slipped off a railway wagon during unloading at Küstrin. His mother, whose father was Polish, was a very imposing figure – very clever, compassionate, with a heart of gold. She was propertied and although she had many proposals of marriage after she was widowed, she could not bring herself to remarry because no one could ever be as good and kind and caring as her beloved Gustav. She had a very hard time bringing up her children after the Great War, but all her children won scholarships for higher education. We saw nothing of her after 1945 as she managed to escape to East Berlin.

Much later, after my father had been released as a POW to the West of Germany, he asked the German Democratic Republic (GDR) authorities for permission to visit her because she had become very ill. Permission was refused. When a telegram arrived to say she had died, he was refused permission to attend her funeral. The reason: there was no point in travelling to Berlin now, as she was dead.

The same happened to my mother in 1983. Her father, my beloved grandfather, died in the GDR. But we lived in West Germany. Permission to attend his funeral was not granted. He was dead. So, why do you want to come to the GDR? To explain: in the early days of the GDR only visits from parents to children were allowed, or children to parents. The rules were relaxed later on. But the paper-work that went with these visits was formidable; every visitor was treated as a potential spy. You had to present yourself at the police station within one hour of arrival, you had to attend 'enlightenment classes', which you did with great enthusiasm – and it was, of course, a great joy for you to bring your relatives as well. Even if you learned nothing, at least the police knew where you were in the evenings. And your relatives better attend these classes as well because if they didn't, they would disappear after you had travelled home, never to be heard of again.

It was virtually impossible to assist our East German relatives in any way. On one occasion my mother took several pairs of tights with her for her sister-in-law. On her way back to the West she was stopped by the GDR police and questioned about the now missing tights. My mother told them that she had thrown them away as they were laddered. 'Next time,' said the friendly policeman, 'bring them back with you.' Point taken. The GDR was leading the world – I have forgotten what in – they needed no assistance with anything and certainly no handouts.

So theoretically you could visit your East German relatives, but the East had exclusion zones, up to 15km and even up to 30km east of the river Elbe, which was the border with the West. And with great foresight old people's homes were opened in those exclusion zones, so that no western spies could infiltrate the minds of the elderly. The regime worked hard to keep them sheltered and safe.

We had been robbed of all our earthly possessions, everything that previous generations had built up was gone. Far worse: most of our much loved immediate family had been cruelly killed in 1945. Now political dogma robbed us of even saying farewell to our remaining nearest and dearest.

I am writing all this from memory. I have not consulted historical records or anything that might help me to reconstruct the events of late 1944 to 1946 and a few years thereafter. I am truthfully recording what I saw and heard and lived through. I saw, obviously, through the eyes of a child and with a child's mind, but I do have a good memory and my observations are historically correct. This is not fiction. This is the truth unfolding.

Although I was very young, a baby really, some events are crystal clear in my mind.

It must have been autumn judging by the colour of the leaves on the trees. My parents had arranged to meet somewhere in the afternoon and I was taken there in the pram by my mother. It must have been a special occasion for my parents, as they talked about it years later. I was overjoyed when I interrupted them and enthusiastically shouted, 'Yes, I remember the place!' and they said, you can't, you were barely one year old and you were in a pram. And I continued delightedly, yes, and the pram was brown and cream and there was a small open travelling circus in a clearing; I described to them a scantily dressed young acrobat performing as a contortionist, announced and given a running commentary by an older compere dressed formally in a black suit. And lots of people laughed and shouted and clapped their hands. My parents looked at me at first in disbelief, but I was their first-born and naturally the most beautiful and cleverest girl in the world. So, if 'Prinzeßchen' said it was like so, then it must have been like so and both parents claimed: 'She takes after me.'

I remember another occasion when I was given my first pair of ankle-high shoes. Children in those days wore high lace-up boots, which made for very weak ankle joints. No one seemed to have realised this. But I walked very early and so well that I was treated to grown up shoes. I walked into the yard which was very large. I walked into the orchard which was even larger. And as you might expect, my feet got tired from the unusual exercise and I twisted my left ankle. I was hurt, I fell and I could not get up. But I did not cry. So sure and aware was I of the security of my home and the loving care of my parents that I only had to sit there where I was, I would be rescued. And indeed, a little later my father came running towards me with arms outstretched, I was picked up and kissed and made a fuss of, a doctor was called, I was bandaged up and spoiled and given a lot of presents the next day – more plasticine, drawing paper, coloured pencils – there was no end to all the goodies and visitors and uncles and aunts with still more presents. I rather liked being injured, but when that was over I was back to high lace-up boots. That was when I was about 16 months old.

Another heartwarming image springs to mind. I remember with great affection sitting on a sand-coloured blanket on the fresh green grass in the garden under a large apple tree covered with pinkish-white blossoms, the sweet scent of them, the buzzing of bumble bees, the jubilant birds, the blue sky, the golden sun, the warm, soft air and the bright yellow dandelions dotted all around me. I see myself laughing and being consciously aware of the joy and beauty of spring; the month must have been May, so I was around 18 months old.

Children were royalty in our household, we were the most important people in the lives of our parents, grandparents and great-grandparents, but our upbringing was what one might call old-fashioned. I call it very strict and what we could do or not do was clearly defined. We could do no wrong. Meaning not outright wrong, better phrased as perhaps not quite right, but never wrong. There was plenty of room for talking and explaining.

Once I was frustrated and as I did not quite understand what was required of me I spoke up and said, 'I cannot help it, I don't yet have the reasoning of a grown-up.' This was quite calmly accepted as a perfectly plausible explanation for my behaviour and my status was almost that of another grown-up engaged in a conversation among equals.

Great-grandmama Gauthier was the grande dame in our family. She was an exceedingly beautiful woman. Her whole demeanour commanded respect. She used to sit on a dais by the window from which she could overlook the entire yard and outbuildings arranged in a rectangle, with the house forming one of the sides. From that window she would supervise the comings and goings of everyone, people and animals alike. You could not reach the front door from the street or from the front field without first having to walk through the yard and you could not come from the fields at the back of the house without walking through the orchard and then through the yard. People always greeted her most respectfully and she ever so slightly bowed her head in acknowledgement.

You were not allowed to call her nana or granny or something that familiar. She was addressed very formally as great-grandmama, followed by her maiden surname. When afternoon came I was allowed to visit her accompanied by my mother. Such a visit was a great honour and was quite a performance. I was washed and combed and polished until I shone, best dress was to be worn, always designed and hand sewn by my father's mother, who was very fashion conscious. We would walk up to her room and knock. We were expected, of course, to be punctual. We were asked in and remained standing at a respectable distance from her dais, my mother within touching distance behind me. Upon a slight push from my mother in my back I would curtsy and wish her 'Good afternoon, Great-grandmama Gauthier.' Then she would say, 'Good afternoon, *mein liebes Kind*, have you had a good day?' I would curtsy again and say 'Yes, thank you Great-grandmama Gauthier.' Then '*Mein liebes Kind*, what have you learnt today?' Upon that I got another push in my back from my mother, took another step forward, curtsied again and recited a verse. A four-liner as a rule. Then she thanked me and wished me good night. '*Schlaf schön und träume süß*' ('sleep well and sweet dreams'). Another curtsy and a thank-you and with that we were dismissed.

My mother never had to suffer the shame of me forgetting my words. Their delivery was practised again and again. While I had my dinner, my mother would sit opposite me at the table with a book, *Verses for Young Children*. She would read some out to me and then

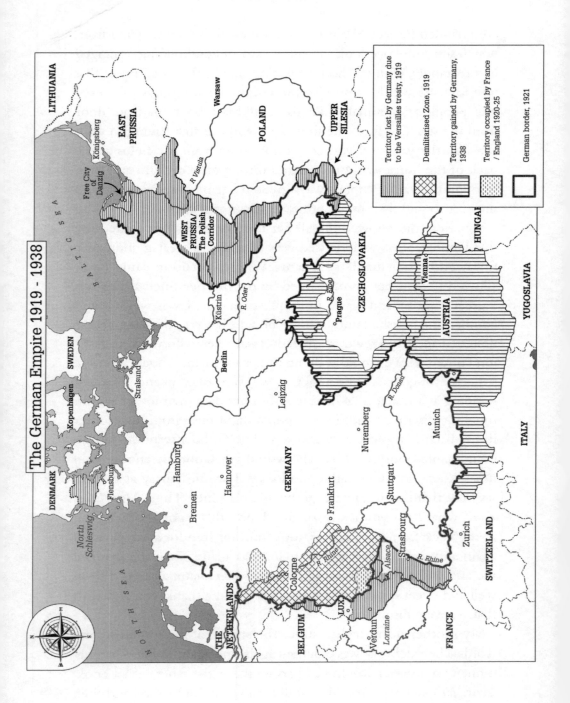

The German Empire 1919 - 1938

Territory lost by Germany due to the Versailles treaty, 1919	Demilitarised Zone, 1919	Territory gained by Germany, 1938	Territory occupied by France / England 1920-25	German border, 1921

we would choose one suitable to be recited in the afternoon. How to curtsy and when to curtsy was also well practised before my early afternoon rest. After all, I was under two years old – but nonetheless well trained for an audience with Great-grandmama Gauthier.

Then there came a day when the house fell silent. There was great sorrow, a lot of people dressed in black arrived, uncles, aunties, people I had never seen before, all in black, some crying. They carried huge bouquets and wreaths in green and white, some had small persons with them, small like me and like me dressed all in white. They were called cousins. That was news to me. I had not known that I was a cousin. It was so exciting. I wandered out of the house and there, like an apparition from a fairy tale, a most beautiful carriage drew up in front of the house, its polished black wood and shining glass sparkling in the bright sunlight. It was drawn by four black horses, the finest I had ever seen, decorated like the carriage with silver ornaments and tassels, wearing black and silver crowns on their heads. It was breathtaking. I was overjoyed and started running back to the house to tell my mother about this truly unbelievable, magnificent sight.

But I was held back; some men, including my father, were walking slowly past me carrying on their shoulders a long, black, shiny box decorated with silver ornaments and masses of white flowers. My great-grandfather walked behind them, crying and I remember clearly him saying, 'I have always held her in the highest esteem.' I did not know what this meant. It sounded as if his heart was speaking for him.

Great-grandmama Gauthier had died. Our family had lost with her a piece of history, a way of life gone forever and I am grateful that I can remember this glimpse of the past. This took place four or five weeks before my second birthday.

After that my grandfather took a great interest in me. The learning of poems continued; there was not a fairy tale I did not know. My grandfather seemed to know all the stories in all the books in all the world. I adored his readings and I placed my foot wherever he took his away.

But life became tough. I had to learn about work. As the future heiress of the property I had to learn all about it: how to look after the land, the animals, the trees, the people, the garden, the fences, and so many more things, not to mention the house itself. I was given my own garden, my own tools. This was not a game. I learnt to graft the cherry tree in my own garden when I was four. But long before even then I was told if ever you ask someone to do a job, know how to do the job yourself. I was instructed to clear a path alongside the house about 12m long; there was a gate at one end. This path was to be cleaned of any bits of straw or whatever should not be there, then raked smooth, showing a proper recognisable pattern, neat and tidy, please. The gate was then to be closed.

The fact that someone later on would have to open the gate again was neither here nor there. My job was: clean path, rake it, close gate at 15.30 and do this promptly and punctually. So, when is 15.30? Typical of our upbringing, there was no task that did not entail the learning of another. My mother was in charge of the time. I was used to her methods of teaching and time was learned on day one of path clearing.

My work was always inspected and favourably commented on by my parents or grandparents and this was quite important to me. I was also rewarded. My work was so good that I was rewarded with lessons in knitting. My first piece of art was not a straightforward piece of flannel or scarf. Oh no, it was one pair of socks requiring the use of five needles. Well, it was just not possible to learn one job without being jollied into learning another. But it made me feel important and quite superior. It was like being given a medal. Better still, I could have some chocolate or jelly babies or pink- and white-striped peppermint. But not as many as I would have liked. Sweets came in restricted quantities.

My grandmother was ready with a toy grocery shop, with scales, weights: 1gm, 10gm, 15gm and a few more. A wooden board and a knife with my name carved on the handle by my great-grandfather. Now I could cut up chocolate. 20gm for myself, 20gm jelly babies for my sister, 20gm chocolate for my grandmother's coffee break and other such delights. I felt like a magnanimous queen giving gifts. I could do even more than that. I could tot up all the gifts I had handed out on each occasion, 20gm + 15 + 25, and so on. For this I was given an abacus with yellow and red beads. I would push these beads about with great enthusiasm; sometimes my gifts worked out to be 80 or even 100gm in one day. I was working so hard. My mother showed me how to write these numbers down on a piece of paper, then I could take this piece of paper and read it out to my grandmother, who said I was very clever, so I could go into the garden and get her three sprigs of marjoram. 'You know the difference between marjoram and parsley, don't you, my dear child?' And the 'dear', now very proud, little child trotted off into the garden to fetch as requested. Had I missed something? Had ulterior motives been at work? I was too innocent to recognise unobtrusive guidance. School? That was still a long way away.

One particular incident delights me still today. I was to be in charge of goslings who had been given a run in the barn annex of about 2.5m x 3.5m that I had to keep clean. Animals living in a proper stable gave me real status. We had large numbers of geese and other animals on our land. But these four goslings were set aside for me to care for. They were to be let out early for grazing and like 'the Little Gänsehirtin' in the fairy tale by the Brothers Grimm, I set off with them even before breakfast, having crept out of bed quietly with a little hazel switch in my hand and a book – quite big and heavy – under my arm. I walked them about in the orchard, the sun shone brightly, it was so warm so early in the day, the goslings ate their fill and nestled down to rest, so I lay down on my tummy and opened my book. It was quite an old edition of Goethe's works and a marker had been put by my grandfather on the page with Goethe's 'Heideröslein'. I read it, I loved it and started learning it by heart. To my great amusement and pleasure the goslings moved closer and started to settle on the open pages and as I learnt the lines I had to keep picking up the soft little creatures, read the verses underneath and quickly memorise them before they moved back onto the pages. I did not know if they had an interest in poetry, perhaps they mistook the shimmering rays of the sun on the white paper for water. I will never forget the wonderful morning when I was in a race with little goslings to see who could get at the print first. I lived an enchanted life.

When I was four, nursery school was considered. My mother took me there in the morning and collected me again in the afternoon. But the experiment got the thumbs down on day three. My mother considered nursery school, after what she had seen of it, as inappropriate and unsuitable for me. 'Far too childish,' was her verdict.

So I had few playmates, but there were those cousins and I had a most beautiful silver-haired little sister with big blue-grey eyes. I also had a tiny brother. I could not see what uses he had as he could not even walk. So I largely ignored him.

My mother's mother was a passionate cook. In her younger days she had worked in a famous Berlin Hotel near the Kaiser's palace. Outside that palace my grandfather was serving as a guard to the Kaiser. To be chosen as a guard was an honour. You received no salary, you provided your own uniform, you came from a good Prussian landed background and your family motto was 'Do more than your duty'. My grandfather fitted the bill. My grandmother often passed him standing outside the palace on duty. Few words could be said between them because of the circumstances. But one day as she walked by, he said: 'Well, Fräulein, when do we get married?' Details were arranged during the following days as they could not speak openly to each other and only a few discreet words could be said as they were in the public eye. But their plans went ahead and my grandparents, once married, moved to the family property east of the Oder.

My grandmother pursued her culinary passion. This meant an awful lot of food was cooked and it had to be eaten. This in turn meant large dinner parties all the time. For me this meant best dress was to be worn every so often. As heiress I did not have to go to bed early, instead I was standing in the line-up in the hall greeting guests and sometimes saying goodbye at ever such a late hour. I was even allowed to sit at the table, having mastered the art of how to hold a fork – quite unlike how it is held today. I was not allowed to drink wine and I considered grown-ups pretty gullible because wine was really sour, unpalatable stuff. I was given elderberry juice. It is so healthy for you but it has its own dangers: never spill it. It stains. I was a very delicate eater and drinker. Small wonder.

I liked the parties, the lampions in the garden, the cheery faces, all the talking and singing and laughing, everyone speaking kindly to me. Often I was asked to recite poems. I was vaguely aware of being some kind of showpiece and I was eager to oblige and actually loved to be praised. I was not so fond of grown-ups' food. You ate what was put on your plate, all of it. You smiled, said thank you and that was that.

Well, the good life did not last. The parties were getting quieter, voices were kept down, sometimes the talk turned into a whisper. Something to do with a party, some undefinable unease and feeling of some kind of danger crept into life.

One day three men arrived to talk to my mother. My grandparents joined in but I was sent out of the room. I became frightened. What had happened was this: my mother had been awarded the Mother's Cross, given in recognition to women with three or more children. My mother did not wear the Mother's Cross; she also cancelled Mother's Day as superfluous. If you want to be good to your mother then you can be good every day of the year, not just on one.

A large picture of a man's head was hung on the main wall of the sitting room. It said underneath '*Unser Führer*'. And a big book was placed in a prominent space on the reception room table. The title was *Mein Kampf*. The picture and the book had been given to my parents on their wedding day as a gift by the registrar and my parents seemed to have forgotten to display this gift in their home. Now they had done so, oil had been poured on troubled waters; all seemed fine. But more officious-looking people arrived talking to everyone in the house about a party and saying that one should be in it, but no one in the whole house was in it. I did not understand any of it, except that it was not a good thing not to be in it. The consequences would affect us in years to come. Little did we know what wrong we had done.

One day two people with two large bags and three little girls arrived on our doorstep. There was much hugging and kissing and crying and questioning. Surprise was shown by everyone in our house. They were clearly much loved and made most welcome. The three little girls were also cousins. I had so many by now. And the grown-ups were a new uncle and auntie I had never seen before. They were going to live with us for a while. It was all so very exciting.

I was not told then what had really happened. But I found out that they had lived south of Danzig, well east of the Oder in Germany. After the Great War that part of Germany had been made over to Poland. This area, populated by Germans for hundreds of years, was now renamed 'The Polish Corridor'. It had changed their lives drastically. They did not want to be Polish. They also believed that this turn of events would not be of long duration. But it was. Years later, when their little girls were of school age, they had to give school a miss because they were stoned on their way there. German women could only go shopping in convoy because of frequent attacks on them by some Poles. They were denied access to a doctor and in winter they were refused coal.

Winters could get very cold where I lived, the ground was frozen up to a whole metre deep, and as mercury freezes at -39°C, no one bothered to look at the thermometer on cold days, it would not tell you more than it was at most -39°C. We wore special clothing in winter, finger gloves inside mittens and then hands were put inside a muff which we children wore on a ribbon round our necks. We also wore double shoes. I really mean it. One pair was made of lined leather and a second pair, a little larger, was pulled over the top. They were called *Galoschen*. They had no laces, they were buttoned.

Not having access to coal and therefore no heating meant your chances of survival were slim in the long run. So my new uncle and aunt had packed two bags with treasured belongings, took their three girls and walked out on their property, their house, their fields, their lives' work and had run for it. Better empty handed but alive.

My uncle was very knowledgeable in the production of certain foods and was soon made manager of a local factory and they all moved into a very, very large house. I loved my new family members, they were all so cheerful and musical. They had such beautiful voices, like almost everyone in my family. Did I mention that all of my family loved opera? There was hardly an aria or duet or a chorus from any opera that I had not heard. My new auntie could go one better: she knew all my little poems and if they had been set to music she would sing them for me. She knew not only the folksong version but also the versions created by famous composers.

How little joy was left for all of us and how short a life for most. Thinking back to that time now, I feel ice-cold terror creeping up on me. What a mercy that we could not look into the future.

SCHOOL

Then in 1939 came the day in early September when I was allowed to go to school. What a highlight of my life. I wore the biggest bow ever in my hair. I had a creaking, squeaking new leather satchel, a gigantic cone-shaped stiffened paper bag in my arms, almost as big as me, the top held together with crêpe paper and a huge bow. It was filled with chocolates and sweets of all kinds and all the family and uncles and aunts accompanied me to school. There we met other children also accompanied by their families and, like me, carrying big, big sweetie bags. We were introduced to our teacher, quite an elderly gentleman who had taught my father when he was a little boy. What an incredible day.

The school building had large rooms with big windows and a huge school yard with very high iron spiked railings all round it. I was used to climbing quite tall trees and saw at a glance that these railings would be hard to climb. I naturally thought that the school yard was for playing in. I could not have been more wrong.

On that first day speeches were made to which I paid no attention. There was too much to see and I was thinking about the contents of my *Schultüte*, which could be opened when I got home as a reward for going to school. Some older children sang for us, which ended my first day of school. I skipped home triumphantly and there I could empty my enormous sweetie bag and distribute all the sweets. It was like dipping into Aladdin's cave. And all because I was so fantastic and clever and had gone to school.

I loved school and all my new friends. I knew the way well and was allowed to go by myself. I did not walk, I ran all the way, even waving my books to show everyone I met that I was a big girl and on my way to school. One day, it was the same September, I was running home; I could not wait to get back to tell everyone what I had learned that day. Halfway home I met my father coming towards me carrying a suitcase. He put it down and laughed and picked me up and swung me round and said, 'Run, little princess, run; run up to the field with the railway line. I am going on a journey. I will be on the train and will wave to you. Everyone is already there waiting for you.'

Now, that was something really exciting. I laughed and waved as he hurried away from me and he waved back until he was round a bend in the road. I arrived breathlessly at the top of our field which was crossed by a railway line. Apart from my immediate family a lot of other people had already gathered there. But they were so quiet. I felt uneasy, something was wrong, why shouldn't you cheer when someone came by on a train and wave? But not so, some older women even cried.

My mother held my sister's hand and had my little brother on her arm. 'Come here, my child and wave when Daddy comes by.' The train arrived. I could not believe so many heads looking out of the windows, so many arms waving. The air was full of voices. I recognised Daddy, laughing and waving. 'Bye bye, keep your beak up, good luck.' And the train disappeared in the distance. Then all was silent, except some women were crying helplessly. I was puzzled. People looked devastated. What was all that about? My mother ushered us home.

Home was strange, also silent, empty. Where was everyone? My uncles all gone. Only my great-grandfather and my grandfather were left. My grandfather was not allowed to go on the train. He had a crippled left arm. He had suffered his injury to his arm in the Great War before I was born. He was in a Prussian regiment with that motto, 'Do more than your duty'. I was always awed by this as it summed my grandfather up so perfectly. All the people who had helped to work the fields had also disappeared, as had all the horses. 'Just like the Great War,' my grandmother said. 'The men and horses go first.'

I did not understand. What was to become of us? I knew enough about farming to grasp immediately the enormity of it. Who would sow the rye and plough the fields and in spring plant the potatoes? How would we get food for ourselves and the remaining animals? My grandfather had about 200 special rabbits. They were chinchillas and needed lots of hay in winter. Who would bring it in from the meadows? Max Schmeling was a friend of my grandfather. He also bred chinchillas and often called at our place. I did not know that he was a famous boxer. He was just uncle Max – and a very jolly uncle he was, who didn't find it beneath him to 'talk rabbit' with a little girl. Anyway, between the two of them they knew someone who knew someone and one day in autumn a large wagon, loaded high with hay, arrived in our yard drawn by two huge Belgian horses. They were 'exempted' horses, whatever that was. And in times to come I became well acquainted with them.

The house became quieter still. All the women went to factories, except my mother. She had more children than the other women in the house and was expecting another. So she was put in charge of all the other children so that their mothers could also go to work. Now all my cousins were her children as well. This meant she had no time to work in the garden or in the fields. This was a disaster. I was very young, but this situation filled me with panic. It meant no food, not for us, not for the animals, for no one.

Then my grandmother was 'enlisted'. She was actually very ill with a heart problem. But the person who had come from the Party said she should work for her Fatherland and also asked whether she expected any pay or whether she would volunteer. I remember her saying to my mother that evening, 'What could I possibly say but just ask for the minimum to pay for essential services?' My grandfather with his crippled arm was also 'volunteered'. That left my mother with nine children in our big house, with me being the eldest, and my great-grandfather. The outlook was more than bleak, like staring into an abyss.

The sting in the tail was this. We were not in the Party. That meant all men not in the Party were called up first to fight for their Fatherland, whether they had one or a dozen children. There was no promotion, so they remained on a private's pay leaving their families in financial distress. Family men were denied leave for Christmas. The disadvantages were accumulative, particularly as Party members were allocated extra food ration cards as a reward for loyalty to the Führer. In later years my mother said, 'We had been downright stupid. Forget principles and high ideals. Of prime importance is to stay alive and bend with the wind and adapt and survive whatever is thrown at you.'

There had been many people who had been cleverer than us, but later it turned out that my mother was a highly intelligent and quick-witted learner and she became a survivor extraordinaire; in a class of her own.

Meanwhile, at school many things changed. My small class of about 22 children became bigger and bigger. More and more desks were crammed into the classroom until we could barely squeeze into our chairs. In the end there were 72 children. It was almost like playing sardines. We found it hilarious when one of our little classmates was not agile enough to reach her desk and had to climb over another desk to get to her chair. That happened so often that it became a routine and was the normal way to reach your place. We did not know that this was an abnormal situation; we were amused by it all and school was really wonderful, the fun we had. Not only that, I was utterly intrigued by the fact that most of the new people could not speak what was called German. They spoke words which we did not understand; now I know it was mainly Dutch, French, Polish and Hungarian. It sparked great interest, enthusiasm and curiosity, for me anyway. We all thought that these various languages were what school was all about. There were many misunderstandings, but we were all good natured about it and it caused hilarity.

I could not get home fast enough to tell my mother all the new words I had learned every day and was determined to learn all the languages in the world. I never did, but I must say we were taught well, very well. An experienced teacher is a joy to have. How ours managed to control us and stimulate our thirst for knowledge I don't know. But in my second year I could decline and conjugate like greased lightning and so could most of my friends. We could do the small and large time tables backwards and forwards and our new school friends learned German in record time.

We were also taught to sing. Not songs as you might think. No, quite formal singing with endless doh, ray, mes, up and down the scale with the appropriate hand movements, again and again. It was so awkward to stand in the narrow space between desk and chair to sing, with the windows open to inhale the fresh air. I wonder what people thought who lived near our school. Perhaps they closed their windows.

My favourite songs were, when allowed to sing, *Märkische Heide*, *Ännchen von Tharau* and *Ich hatt' einen Kameraden*.

> Märkische Heide, Märkischer Sand
> Sind des Märkers Freude,
>
> Sind sein Heimatland.
> Steige hoch, du roter Adler,
>
> Hoch über Sumpf und Sand,
> Hoch über dunkle Kiefernwälder,
>
> Heil dir mein Brandenburger Land.
>
> Uralte Eichen, Dunkler Buchenhain,

Grünende Birken stehen am Wiesenrain.
Steige hoch, du roter Adler,
Hoch über Sumpf und Sand, Hoch
über dunkle Kiefernwälder,
Heil dir mein Brandenburger Land.

Blauende Seen, Wiesen und Moor,
Liebliche Täler, Schwankendes Rohr.

Steige hoch, du roter Adler,
Hoch über Sumpf und Sand, Hoch
über dunkle Kiefernwälder,
Heil dir mein Brandenburger Land.

Knorrige Kiefern leuchten im Abendrot,
Sah'n wohl frohe Zeiten, Sah'n auch
märk'sche Not. Steige hoch,
du roter Adler, Hoch über Sumpf und Sand,
Hoch über dunkle Kiefernwälder,
Heil dir mein Brandenburger Land.

Bürger und Bauern vom märk'schen Geschlecht,
Hielten stets in Treu zur märk'schen Heimat fest!
Steige hoch, du roter Adler, Hoch über Sumpf und Sand,
Hoch über dunkle Kiefernwälder,
Heil dir mein Brandenburger Land.

Hie Brandenburg allewege - Sei unser Losungswort!
Dem Vaterland die Treue in alle Zeiten fort.
Steige hoch, du roter Adler,
Hoch über Sumpf und Sand,
Hoch über dunkle Kiefernwälder,
Heil dir mein Brandenburger Land.

Brandenburg Heath, Mark Brandenburg sand
Are the joy of the Märker, are his homeland.
Climb high, you red eagle, over bog and sand,
High above the dark pine forests,
Hail to my Brandenburger country.
Ancient oaks, dark beech wood,
Green birch trees lining the meadow.
Climb high, you red eagle,
High above marsh and sand,
Above the dark pine forests,
Hail to my Brandenburger country.
Blue lakes, meadows and marsh,
Lovely valleys, swaying reed beds.
Climb high, you red eagle,
High above marsh and sand,
Above the dark pine forests,
Hail to my Brandenburger country.
Knotty pine trees in the sunset glow,
They have seen most joyful times
Have also seen Brandenburg's hardships,
Fly high you red eagle, over marsh and sand,
High above the dark pine forests,
Hail to my Brandenburger country.
Citizens and peasants from mark Brandeburg's lineage,
Always hold true to your homeland!
Climb high, you red eagle, over bog and sand,
High above the dark pine forests,
Hail to my Brandenburger country.
Brandenburg here evermore – be our watchword!
Loyalty to the Fatherland continue for all time.
Climb high, you red eagle, over bog and sand,
High above the dark pine forests,
Hail to my Brandenburger country.

Ännchen von Tharau (Friedrich Silcher)

Ännchen von Tharau ist, die mir gefällt,
sie ist mein Leben, mein Gut und mein Geld.
Ännchen von Tharau hat wieder ihr Herz
auf mich gerichtet in Lieb und in Schmerz.
Ännchen von Tharau, mein Reichtum, mein Gut,
du meine Seele, mein Fleisch und mein Blut.

Käm alles Wetter gleich auf uns zu schlahn,
wir sind gesinnt beieinander zu stahn.
Krankheit, Verfolgung, Betrübnis und Pein
soll unsrer Liebe Verknotigung sein.
Ännchen von Tharau, mein Reichtum, mein Gut,
du meine Seele, mein Fleisch und mein Blut.

Recht als ein Palmenbaum über sich steigt,
hat ihn erst Regen und Sturmwind gebeugt,
so wird die Lieb in uns mächtig und groß
nach manchem Leiden und traurigem Los.
Ännchen von Tharau, mein Reichtum, mein Gut,
du meine Seele, mein Fleisch und mein Blut.

Würdest du gleich einmal von mir getrennt,
lebtest da, wo man die Sonne kaum kennt;
ich will dir folgen durch Wälder und Meer,
Eisen und Kerker und feindliches Heer.
Ännchen von Tharau, mein Licht, meine Sonn,
mein Leben schließt sich um deines herum.

Little Annie of Tharau

Little Annie of Tharau is the one I like best,
she is my life, my riches and wealth.
Little Annie of Tharau has once more turned
her heart towards me in love and in pain.
Little Annie of Tharau, my riches, my wealth,
you are my soul, my own flesh and blood.

If storms and foul weather should threaten us dire,
our intent would still be to stand by each other.
Sickness, persecution, sadness and pain
would tie fast the knots of love for us twain.
Little Annie of Tharau, my riches, my wealth,
you are my soul, my own flesh and blood.

Just as the palm tree will grow to full height
once rain and storms have tempered its might,
just so will our ardour grow tall and strong
after suffering and sorrow have let it alone.
Little Annie of Tharau, my riches, my wealth,
you are my soul, my own flesh and blood.

If we had to part and you had to live where
hardly is known the warmth sunshine can give,
still would I seek you through forest and sea,
nor irons nor foes could keep me from thee.
Little Annie of Tharau, my light and sunshine,
my life enfolds yours, as yours enfolds mine.

Ich hatt' einen Kameraden   *I Had a Comrade*
von Ludwig Uhland   (Translation by Frank Petersohn)

Ich hatt' einen Kameraden,	In battle he was my comrade,
Einen bessern findst du nit.	None better I have had.
Die Trommel schlug zum Streite,	The drum called us to fight,
Er ging an meiner Seite	He always on my right,
In gleichem Schritt und Tritt.	In step, through good and bad.
Eine Kugel kam geflogen:	A bullet it flew towards us,
Gilt's mir oder gilt es dir?	For him or meant for me?
Ihn hat es weggerissen,	His life from mine it tore,
Er liegt vor meinen Füßen	At my feet a piece of gore,
Als wär's ein Stück von mir	As if a part of me.
Will mir die Hand noch reichen,	His hand reached up to hold mine.
Derweil ich eben lad.	I must re-load my gun.
"Kann dir die Hand nicht geben,	"My friend, I cannot ease your pain,
Bleib du im ew'gen Leben	In life eternal we'll meet again,
Mein guter Kamerad!"	And walk once more as one."

School did get curiouser still. We learned a new handwriting. It was called 'Latin' and it made my name look totally different from the angular German version. In retrospect I am surprised how fast we learned the new style. There were a lot of new letters to be learned and the emphasis was on neatness and proper proportions; absolutely essential because in German a word starting with a small letter means something totally different from a word starting with a capital letter but otherwise has the same spelling. And care is required when writing the articles. The noun that follows it can mean something quite different depending on the article that precedes it. We managed very well and were only about eight years old.

My mother was very busy with so many young children to look after, so my grandmother supported me after she came home from work. She wanted me to teach her what I had learned that day.

The evenings were glorious. My grandfather joined us at the table as well and I was eager to show off my new skills. My grandfather narrated Greek sagas, stories about the old Romans, the Egyptians; he talked about hieroglyphics, the runes, about the Chinese, the constellations in the sky; there was no end to all the truly wonderful things in the world. There was not only German handwriting and Latin and Greek and Russian, there were more and more ...

I could not wait to grow up, then I would go and see all the places that were then just dreams to me. But those dreams would turn into paralysing nightmares. In spite of all this, I would manage to survive and would still go on learning new words, new languages. We did not know that then.

History, local history, I found fascinating. Once our class was taken for a long walk to a neighbouring village to see a brickworks. The works manager, who took us round and who did the explaining, laughed loudly when he saw 70-odd children snaking through the works. He was good-humoured and seemed to take a great interest in me, even took me by my hand, it felt like a private personal tour of the works.

When I described at home all the things I had seen my great-grandfather and my grandmother laughed and explained that the brickworks had once been family property. In fact, our very high, spacious barn had been built from bricks manufactured there. My great-grandfather's brother-in-law had been a very successful businessman. He owned the brickworks; but he also had a great weakness. He was a poacher. Although he had more than enough money to buy as much venison or whatever else that lived in the forest as he liked, it had to be secretly and illegally acquired. The forester suspected him, the police suspected him. His house was searched every so often, but they never managed to link him to a vanished deer or boar. The forester knew every animal in his *revier* and a shot could be overheard. So he and the police were always ready to pursue the phantom poacher.

One day this poacher relative came running from the forest with a freshly killed young red deer and shouted to his wife to be quick, because he was closely followed. They had a new baby who was lying in a cradle in one of the rooms. So our quick-thinking poacher whipped the mattress away from under the baby, put in the deer, draped a blanket over it and put the now bawling baby on top. At that point two policemen burst through the door demanding to search the house. 'No problem,' but with his wife being busy in the kitchen and the baby ill, would one of the policemen kindly rock the cradle, then he would go round with the other police-man searching the house? Agreed. The baby, clearly uncomfortable, bawled louder and louder so the search was curtailed and none was happier than the policeman who was rocking the baby and the deer to get out of there.

That was not the end of it. Our charming relative went round to the police station a little later and reported a gold pocket watch missing. It had been in a wardrobe drawer in the baby's room and the only outsider who had been in this room that day had been the baby rocking policeman. It caused a rumpus; but neither the deer nor the gold watch was ever found.

The wife of this poacher was getting more and more angry about having her home searched by the police every so often. One day during an argument she hit her husband over the head with the frying pan. In her haste and fury she had forgotten to wait for the fried bacon, hot fat and glowing pan to cool down before she whacked him and he sustained serious injuries. That started a war between them. They both employed solicitors and continued war-ring for a few years. This depleted their resources and the factory had to be sold. At this stage they came to their senses and both found their marriage worth saving. So they decided to start a new life together with their two little boys and with the remainder of their money they emigrated to America.

My great-grandfather and grandmother accompanied them to Hamburg and waved them off on a big ocean steamer. My grand-mother recalled that her auntie did not wear shoes but a pair of *Höltentinen*. This is, I believe, a mangled Dutch-German word for wooden slippers. The soles are carved from wood and they have leather uppers. That's how they left Germany, ill-shod and with little money after paying their fare.

They wrote back and kept in touch with great-grandfather. They were a proud family, undaunted and hard working. One of their sons became a doctor, the other a solicitor. They all lived in New York and great-grandfather had their address. He gave it to my mother in February 1945. I will come to that later.

In connection with the brickworks, I remember something else as told to me by my grandfather and others. The wages for the working men were taken to them by Johann, who collected the money from the local *Volksbank* on a Saturday and he took it to the factory in a bag on his bicycle. One Saturday there was no pay. Johann had disappeared. There was consternation and all sorts of rumours circulated. Then his body, hidden in bushes, was found near the road that he regularly took. He had been ambushed, coshed and blindfolded. His blindfold was partially pulled off and the police assumed that he must have seen his attacker and recognised him. At this point his throat had been cut. His murderer was still at large.

My grandfather was an extremely clever and shrewd man, a very sensitive judge of character. Often people would ask him to read their fortunes from cards. He sometimes obliged and legend has it that he was never wrong. Actually, he could not tell anyone's fortune from cards, but he listened to people and asked questions with his amused smile and knowing him, it meant 'I think I have got the hang of you and I know what makes you tick.' He would then, usually surrounded by people in a *Konditorei* (a pâtisserie/café), shuffle the cards, lay them out on the table and tell a person what lay in store for them. His assessment of people was pretty accurate, no wonder his reputation was high – obviously, his cards told the truth.

One day during a party at such a *Konditorei* he was asked again to read the cards. Guests took their turns and the tension and expectation were as usual very high. They all crowded round him keenly looking at the cards on the table – of which he took no notice, because he did not believe in this nonsense – they were all waiting in silence for the magic words he would utter. Then it was the turn of a man who did not want his fortune told as he did not believe in such hocus-pocus. But the onlookers insisted and he was cajoled into having his cards read. My grandfather shuffled the cards, laid them out on the table and remained silent. 'Go on,' people said, 'what's the delay? What do the cards say?' My grandfather shook his head, gathered up the cards and said, 'I can't believe it. I must have made a mistake.' He shuffled the cards again, laid them out again and looked at them in silence. After a while into the silence of the room he announced calmly: 'The cards say, you murdered Johann.'

Such was my grandfather's reputation that the police were called immediately; the man in question was so shaken that he confessed there and then. His case was heard in Berlin and subsequently he spent the rest of his life in a prison there. I believe it was in Berlin-Spandau. My grandfather admitted that he had been very daring, the murdered person had been known to him for many years, so had his murderer, and my grandfather had used his judgement of human nature and had put two and two together. He never read cards again.

Back at school I gained a new friend. Her name was Theresia. She was Hungarian. Initially she spoke little German but she liked dancing and dancing was my passion. I had never before met anyone who had shared my enthusiasm. At school we entertained the other children during break and we anticipated each other's movement and delighted in dancing together or dancing solo.

She showed me new dances, the Mazurka and *Csardas*. How many people know nowadays how to dance these? I loved to waltz, we would invent our own movements and always had most of the children in the school yard watching, including our teachers. To me a waltz is not exuberant swirling around and swaying into the music. A waltz is a volcano with the lid firmly screwed down. Discipline and being firmly in control shows off the waltz, strength and the balance of line and movement make for its elegance. With the large audience we had at school it was easy to organise all into taking part in a polonaise. Theresia's knowledge of Hungarian and Polish dances was remarkable. She is impossible to forget. Music? We did our own singing or used a harmonica. Oh, glorious times.

Once, with a school friend whose name I have now forgotten, I organised a theatrical performance to take place in their barn with the large barn doors acting as curtains. Almost all the children in the neighbourhood had parts in the performance, singing, reciting poems or acting in little plays, very short plays; the main show was dancing. To our repertoire we had also added a shoe-*plattler*, taught to us by a girl who had come from Tirol.

As for music, well, that was difficult. In fact, it was primitive. People from the Party had been round to collect musical instruments to entertain the troops. So no one had anything to play with or on. Our own piano had gone and we were not given permission to use petrol to transport the big Flügel from one of my aunties to our house so that I could learn to play. But we were inventive. We could play the paper and comb. And if you have several people playing the comb harmonica, then, hey presto, there you have your orchestra. It can only be topped by a cat chorus. I was not in the orchestra. I was the dancing department, with dresses made out of multi-coloured crêpe paper, all cut out and glued together by myself. It was all tremendous fun.

On the day of the performance I went round to my friend in the morning to see whether we would need more chairs or whether we would be allowed to use bundles of straw to sit on for the audience. With so many neighbours saying that they would attend we wanted to avoid standing. And straw was more precious than chairs.

To my mortification I found their home locked; no one in the yard, in the garden or anywhere. I ran home and, greatly upset, told my mother. She listened very quietly, then said, 'You better run round and tell everyone the performance is cancelled, perhaps someone has been taken ill in the family. I will find out and tell you when I come back.'

That evening I was told that their relatives in the Rheinland had been bombed out and that my little friend's family had decided to visit them. What? The entire family had moved away overnight without leaving a message with anyone, to stay with bombed-out relatives who no longer had a house? Would it not have been better if the bombed-out family had moved to our town? No one ever came back – I know they were not Jewish. And they were not the only family that 'moved away' overnight.

I felt a certain nervousness creeping in to my mother's behaviour and my grandmother in particular. But then my grandmother worked in a factory where they made parachutes and if you made a mistake you would die. No wonder she was nervous and I loved her very much and did not want her to die; so I also became nervous.

The school yard where we danced and where I thought on my first day at school we would play, became detestable. We had to learn to march, in rows of four, we had to learn to line up according to height on an imaginary line and all that in double quick time, at the blow of a whistle: '*In einer Linie der Größe nach angetreten*.' I still cannot get this command out of my head. For those that know some German, note that '*antreten*' is an instruction to be followed, but insert a 'ge' between the prefix and the verb then the word is turned into a command that *must* be followed. These almost daily commands became the bane of my life and seemed to hang over my head like the sword of Damocles. The daily drill was OK if only your own class was involved – you quickly learned who to stand next to – but it did get difficult when two or three classes were mixed together at short notice.

We marched and marched in lines of four or two or six straight on, then turned at a 90-degree angle without getting out of line and out of step and we had to sing to a proper rhythm: *links, zwei, drei*, and *links, zwei, drei*, (left, two three) and so on. We hated it and my teacher, whom I loved so much because he cared for us so much, looked strangely tired, sad and quiet. He was an outstanding teacher and a member of the Party, like all public employees. You could not be a teacher, a nurse, a midwife, a doctor, or dentist or shopkeeper or road sweeper or shovel coke at the gasworks or work on the railway, or whatever, unless you were in the Party.

THINGS GO WRONG

There seemed to be a two-tier system in place, one for Party members and one for 'non-believers'. The first group had the advantage of extra rations and a clothes allowance. I remember two people called at our home to inspect the contents because my mother had made a request to renew some curtains for the blackout. Her request was turned down. Curtain material was only for members.

Food rations were a worry for my mother. As the only young and reasonably fit person in our house she managed the entire large property on her own, procured food and cooked for all, including our relatives who worked long hours in factories and appreciated some food when they came home late. Then there were all the children, the washing, the cleaning, the animals, the garden and the fields. Work parties were made up of decrepit old people organised to grow potatoes and vegetables for ourselves and the animals. Logging parties had to be organised; how would you cook or keep the house warm if you had no firewood? She excelled as head of the entire family and her word was law. There were some situations in which even she could not win. There were reduced ration cards for bread and none for milk. Tricky when there are nine children in the house. If you were landed, you had to feed yourself. Problem number one: there were no able-bodied men to work the fields. Problem two: there were no horses, only shared ones on a rota basis. Problem three: every so often animals such as cattle, sheep, goats, pigs, etc, were confiscated for the troops. So you had no ration cards and no animals you could slaughter for meat either. At that stage my mother swapped household belongings for food. It safeguarded the children at least.

In short, and with hindsight, not being in the Party showed you up for what you were – stupid. To be in the Party did not mean that you were a Nazi, but it enhanced your chances of survival. There were always some people who had to learn the hard way.

I was very hard-worked. There was school and after school all the homework. My mother would not accept that her daughter would be second best in anything. The only grade I could bring home was a grade one. Once I brought home a grade two in maths. I was scolded severely. And then there was so much work to do around the house and garden. The aforementioned horses lent to us were my domain. And I felt quite competent with them, because they are lovely, beautiful and clever creatures. If you click your tongue, flick your reins, shout 'hü' and 'hott' and 'whoa' in the right places then they will start or stop, go faster or slower, turn right or left. They also had the most beautiful eyes. But I never managed to reverse them in the yard.

Once someone brought them round into our yard without their gear. We had our own hanging in the barn so I went and fetched it. It was ever so heavy and the horses were ever so tall. Their heads were towering above me. I fetched one of the sawing horses and hanging on to the lovely mane with one hand, I climbed up and tried to pull up the heavy harness with my other hand. I could not. Bran was to be collected from the mill and flour in exchange for the corn we had sent in the week before. The food for the animals and ourselves was at stake. At first I swallowed hard and bravely tried and tried again to pull up the heavy harness. It was hopeless. I couldn't. The lovely, patient horses shook their big heads and I clutched the blonde mane of one of them and burst into helpless tears. His long, light blonde mane stirred some kind of memory in me. I am not sure, but those horses could have been Brabants, Belgian heavy horses.

Just when I thought there was no end to my misery and despair there was a glimmer of hope. By then there were a number of POWs working for us. They came to us in ones or twos or little groups in the morning, always by themselves and they walked back in the evening to their camp as and when they finished. My mother was grand with broken Polish, French and German, working out in the mornings who was to do what, where and when. The POWs were all very friendly and helpful and I always felt that they liked my mother and most tried in every way to be of assistance. We had a very good relationship with them and they seemed to like to come to us. My mother treated all people as equals and she always told us specifically that they were as unhappy as we were, separated from our fathers, sons and brothers. But there was a war on and we had to make the best of it. The POWs did the same. There was little point in running away, perhaps getting lost or starving, or getting shot, although from where we lived you could walk into the forest and without leaving it, you could walk right through to Siberia. But what would be the point of that if you could stay in your camp, go out and work on a farm, get your food, be out of the cold at night, sit out the war, hope for the best and get back to your family again at the end of it? A forlorn hope for most of us, but that hope kept us going.

Some of the regulars became close friends of ours; secretly, of course, as you were not allowed to be friendly with POWs, but it is only human that you feel at ease with some people, trusting them and caring for them as if they were members of your own family. What does it matter that they are of a different nationality? The main problem is the language barrier. Sign language, a friendly face and careful, attentive waiting for the response of the other person and interpreting the response kindly, with good will and imagination, is what one is left with. Sometimes it does not work out but it is important to show friendliness and good will.

As I was crying my eyes out slumped over one of the horses, one of the Polish POWs walked into the yard and seeing my distress came over to me to find out what was wrong. He had friendly eyes and I recognised him as one of our regulars and to me he was just another kind uncle. He came from a farming family and summed up my situation at a glance. My predicament was resolved in minutes and I was a happy girl when I left the yard with wagon and horses to fetch the food from the mill. I was always mindful of the reality that I was not the best person for the job, but in the circumstances that was all we had. Just little me.

At school we continued what is generally known as square bashing. We were something like guards of honour and during and outside school hours we were required to line the streets or the market place when others marched as well. We had to stand in line and look respectful, sometimes we had to back some singing, other times we had to sing before someone made a long speech, (some seemed everlasting), we had to sing at the end of the speeches, then march back to school to be dismissed. Life was turning into a disappointment for me and into a bitter struggle for my mother. She really had her work cut out and her working hours were getting longer. Our supportive marching, flag waving and singing also took place in the evenings in our third year at school. In the dark, with people carrying torches, march to this factory, march to that factory, support a rally here or there and sing your little heart out at the drop of a hat. And my mother and other mothers had no other choice but to go out in the dark as well, as they could hardly abandon their children in a strange part of the town half way through the night. I noticed that my mother was getting tight lipped. She was not in the habit of beating about the bush, but she seemed to be biting her tongue. Conversations between her, my grandparents and my great-grandfather took place in hushed voices with sideways glances at us children to check whether we were listening.

I remember the day when I was doing homework with my grand-mother in their wing of the house in the evening, with boarded-up windows and a cloth thrown over the lamp to dim the light. My grandmother was learning English with me. The four new words we were learning that evening were: flag, mat, cat and bag. The radio was playing quietly and my grandfather studied a fruit tree cata-logue. He was a great tree lover. Suddenly he put down his book, leant back in his chair and called out: '*Du großer Gott.*' I did not know then what disaster had taken place or what caused the consternation in our house and the desperate voices in my grandmother's kitchen, where everyone had suddenly assembled.

Later I learned that had been the day when the Führer had declared war on the Soviet Union. Things seemed to go wrong for us. Our surname was wrong. It was not Aryan. That was seri-ous. I knew names had to be right. But in what way? We had a visitor at school. She explained that we had not descended from the Neanderthals and that it was wrong to do so. And that it was also wrong to descend from Christians and that my name was wrong and that my sister's name was wrong because they were Christian names. I was getting quite afraid; we had a picture of a Neanderthal hanging on the classroom wall but I did not know what a Christian looked like. It was quite a relief when I was given a piece of paper with Aryan names on it to take home to my mother, so that she could choose one for my new baby brother. My mother looked at me for a long time and told me that I had the most beautiful name.

Well, if she said so, I felt reassured, and my Daddy was in the war and she was my protector. So there. With my background I had, of course, a lot of trouble with being Aryan, but then I was in good company. Herr Adolf Hitler and Herr Joseph Göbbels had the same problems, but then they were in the Party and I was not. And that made a difference; in fact, all the difference. And by the way, my mother did not choose a name from that arrogant list for my brother.

Research showed that our surname was a very old German name and I remember that my mother hardly spoke to the com-mittee members who called at our house to tell us so. I found her behaviour rather haughty but heard her say to her mother that evening that she could barely utter a word because she was frozen with fear and so resorted to a kind of superior silence.

The shortage of food was beginning to have an effect. I noticed at school that my sandwiches were stolen. I also saw who took them. I told my mother. 'Well,' she said, 'I am glad you told no one else, and that little girl must have been very hungry. From tomorrow I will give you as many sandwiches as we can afford and you will share your food with others that have nothing to eat.' My sandwiches consisted of home-made bread of varying quality depending on what flour was available, spread with lard fried up with the odd onion and apples and made more palatable with fried marjoram and thyme. From that next day on I took extra food to school to share with others; as my mother said, all people are like us, they have one head, two arms and two legs like we do, they feel hot and cold like we do and they get hungry like we do and you must help your fellow human beings. Well, I tried my best. I was in charge of the sandwiches and it was up to me to decide who would get them. I may have made mistakes, I don't know. I gave them to the children who clearly had nothing to eat at break time. Some children would bring sandwiches, others would not. As I said, I tried my best.

Then food got scarcer still. The POW camps had as good as none. So we and others were allocated a number of POWs to feed every day. Eight to ten men daily. Now the pressure was really on. We were basically down to potatoes. Potato soup, potato soup, every day potato soup. My mother managed to trade goat's milk with the butcher, who let us have pigs' heads, sometimes only ears, tails and trotters. Occasionally sheep's heads, lungs, more rarely liver. Fried liver was really classy. Sometimes we feasted. We had boiled potatoes in their jackets. It was my job to make nests of nettle cloth at intervals on the table and the boiled potatoes were put in there. The steam was absorbed by the cloth, which kept the potatoes dry and hot and everyone had to peel their own with short, pointed potato knives.

The main table seated 14 and there were two tables by the windows for the children. We and the POWs were all treated alike, the same china and best cutlery as we had used for our parties just a few short years ago. It was just the food on our plates that was different. The highlight of the boiled potato feast was the salted herring, still available if you had something to barter with. My mother had an arrangement with the fishmonger where he would let us have the herring that had been in touch with the wood inside the big barrel. The herring in close contact with the wood was always tainted with the taste of wood and was discoloured, a bit brownish. But it was a feast.

Chicken and eggs were no longer available, all of ours and those of neighbouring properties had been stolen long before. The worst was that without the cocks, the hens and their eggs, there were no new chickens. They had become an extinct species. Good table manners were observed by all. I was in charge of one of the children's tables, quite an elevated position. My senior position entitled me to ask at the end of the meal whether it was now over; when my mother answered yes, all remained seated but we children were allowed to lick our plates. I was no longer child enough to use my tongue but wiped my plate clean using my finger. Nothing would go to waste or into the washing up. Once I remember my brother asking, 'Mummy, can we go to bed now before we get hungry again?'

On Sundays we had peeled potatoes and I had to contribute to the preparations of those quartered potatoes, theoretically enough for about 32 people, including the POWs. There was so much to be prepared. My share of the work was to fill a 10-litre white enamel bucket. It had a blue rim. It took me a long time to fill it and I had to peel the potatoes very thinly, although all the peels were boiled for the rabbits, who needed to eat as well. I had been brought up with work and taking on more than one task at a time and it was quite normal for me while sitting on the barn step peeling away dutifully to see my mother run up with a book. She was very busy herself and had little time even to speak to me. But there was now Religion of all the things on my new timetable at school and she could not tolerate the thought that I might not shine in this subject. So she brought along the book with the Ten Commandments, which I could learn while peeling potatoes. Of course I could, that was only natural. No sooner had my mother gone when I saw my grandfather hurrying towards me with another book. I should not get depressed or despondent doing only a manual job, he said, so he had selected a poem by Gottfried Keller for me to learn by heart to keep my spirits up. Very well and thank you very much. I was so practised at learning by heart that by the time the bucket was full the other two missions had also been accomplished and after dinner I could recite, to the satisfaction and enjoyment of my grandfather, my mother and myself, the pieces they had set for me.

Yes, I was a very busy girl and getting busier still. When I was 10 I joined the BDM – *Bund Deutscher Mädel*. If you were a boy you joined the HJ – *Hitler Jugend*. That was automatic. There was no get-out clause and you could not *not* be in it. We wore a white blouse and a very dark skirt. I don't remember whether it was black or a very dark blue. It is of no interest to me, that's why I don't remember. It so happens that I dislike these colours, they are not me, they are perhaps not to any child's liking. Children are made of lively, creative material. We just looked uniform and unimaginative. Uniform is stifling not only for children. It dumbs people down and helps to deprive them of their natural intuitive expression of thoughts and dreams and exploration of the world and the people around them. When robbed of a worthwhile existence in the here and now, children are capable of creating new worlds in their minds and can live in these worlds as if they were real. Sadly, under the Hitler regime the dumbing down had reached a level where so much cold water was poured over the sparks that most were extinguished. But not all; some were smouldering to reignite later. I myself discovered a rebellious streak in me. But at that stage I could not define it or see its origins. I was just going through a rather obstinate phase but could not put my finger on the reason.

The marching and singing and flag waving now continued in uniform. It took so much time out of our lives. There was school, all the hard work at home, in the garden, in the fields, the school homework.

On top of this came the collection of herbs, a certain number of kilos of wild strawberry leaves, of raspberry leaves, of woodruff (a sweet-smelling plant used for flavouring, its German name *Waldmeister* would translate as 'master of the woods') and others. These had to be handed in every week to our unit headquarters, no excuses. We had to turn up for sports afternoons twice a week, at least once a week for orienteering classes where we had to 'outwit our enemy' and turn up at a certain location within a certain time. We were treated as 'traitors' if we did not meet the target and then had to run around a sports field as punishment. I was thinking all the time of my dear mother and who would help her water the carrots and beans, whilst I was running around in woodland like a frightened rabbit, worried sick. To top it all, I felt rejected by my group of young girls in the BDM. Some girls were promoted to lead about ten girls. I was never chosen, although I felt that I was better at organising and cleverer than most; but I had no hope of promotion and I did not know why. I would never make the grade because no one in our family was in the Party. Surprise, surprise – members only.

It was also my duty as a BDM girl to assist Party members with the collection of blankets, clothing, shoes, food and whatever else to help our soldiers and refugees. I spent many hours doing the donkey work of pulling a cart loaded high with goods of all kinds and delivering it all to the town hall for not so much as a thank you, because it was a duty which was to be performed unquestioned. We were also asked to collect food from people for refugees. That was a hard task. Perhaps a bottle of home-made fruit juice? Or a jar of jam? There was a problem. If you gave away a glass bottle or a glass jar full of something then you were now short of a glass bottle or glass jar yourself. There was no hope of a replacement of these valuable items and then you had no means of preserving anything for yourself. So, most of the time the answer to a request for food was a definite no; and we knew why.

Once I was allocated to a team collecting clothing in my own neighbourhood. I knocked at my own front door, curtsied politely and said my piece as prescribed. My mother and grandfather were there.

They gave me the best that was in our wardrobes: my mother included her brand new winter coat, I had accompanied her many times to the local tailor for the fittings and my grandfather included his brand new, warm *paletot*. Was I proud! My family did not give away old clothes or surplus garments. No, my family gave away the best clothes they had, they gave away gifts that were a real sacrifice. I understand now, they did it for me. I will never forget their action and the pride and admiration for them that arose in me because I belonged to this family. I was special, because my family was special.

Whenever I could I visited my cheerful aunt Betty, she always spoiled me and I so loved seeing her. But lately I was not allowed into her kitchen, where she seemed to have people for dinner at odd times and these people did not seem to like to be disturbed. As a polite little girl I never asked why and was happy to amuse myself in the playroom of her three daughters, who had been called up to work as land girls.

Then like a bolt out of the blue my uncle, aunt Betty's husband, was arrested. His crime: he had allowed POWs who worked at his factory to take away small packets of glucose tablets. He had not been betrayed by one of his German workers, no, the POWs had been grassed up by another POW in their camp. When there is an acute shortage of food some people will not hesitate to do the dirty on their fellow sufferers hoping for favours from their guards. We were mortified. There was talk at the trial that he would be shot as a traitor, after all, the glucose tablets were meant for German soldiers. But my uncle succeeded in talking himself out of his potentially mortal predicament. Without a modicum of food for his workers, he said, he could not get any work out of them and without their ability to work to a kind of minimum standard absolutely no one would benefit. And as his expertise in his field could not be obtained from anyone else, he was allowed to return to his post, particularly as production had come to a stop during his time of arrest. And my auntie's dinner parties? Well, they were the people that my uncle had sent up to her secretly to have a bite to eat. It may not have been more than oatmeal cooked in salt water, but it was 100 per cent better than nothing and could make the difference between life and death.

I was only ten years old then and I knew without being told, or should I say warned, that I must not even think about what was happening in Aunt Betty's kitchen in case my thoughts would be read and I would be shot. I started leading a life in fear.

The screw that was hunger and angst was tightening. Our front fields were confiscated, temporary homes were erected, suddenly hundreds of people were living where there had once been rye and potato fields. Our town trebled in size: where there had been approximately 8,000 inhabitants in 1939 there were now 23,000 in 1944 and the numbers were swelling dramatically by the day. There were refugees, mainly from the east, and bombed-out people from all parts of Germany.

For we who farmed the land, work became incredibly hard, in fact, almost impossible. The land nearby was now built upon. The land far away was harder and more time-consuming to reach. There were few or no horses. Manpower was the POWs. They had enough common sense to see that the best policy was to work with us hand in glove, only that way did we all have a chance to survive. You don't last long without food and drink, and there is little time during which you can actively influence your destiny.

Fortunately, we had a good relationship with our POWs. They treated us as family, as we regarded them as members of our family. They shared their worries about their lost families with us. My mother never failed to listen with great sympathy, always expressing hope and desperately wishing that one day the world would be a better place. She was quite alone really and I felt so sorry for her. One of her brothers was missing in Russia, another would be later on at Monte Cassino. My father had not been heard of since El Alamein. My grandmother was very ill with a heart complaint but not excused factory work (no doctor was allowed to issue a sick note), my grandfather with his useless arm was quite arthritic and barely able to crawl to work at the saw mill. Her only support was my great-grandfather, who was well over 80 years of age. He rose to the occasion, always ready to help, even hanging out the washing, very hard for someone almost bent double with age and arthritis.

But when something was to be done, he was already there doing it, quite cheerfully. He was our last line of defence. How cruel life is. What a spine chilling, ghastly end awaited him.

As food got scarcer, we got thinner. I remember my brothers and sister and cousins with stick arms and knobbly knees and huge, hungry eyes. I felt worked to a standstill. Now it was also my duty to deliver so and so many hundredweight of acorns and chestnuts and beechnuts to the Party headquarters. This was a grave development. I was the only working 'man' left in the family. Our own animals needed these very acorns, chestnuts and beechnuts that I had to collect from places far away, as there was no animal food for sale. I had no time for anything any more.

It was not just my family that grew more and more angry. People mentioned words like civil war and public disobedience. What all this meant I could not interpret with my limited experience of life. But I sensed it was something very nasty and dangerous.

One day my dear old teacher asked me to send my mother round to his home. I did and with a bad conscience. I had kept a few baskets of acorns behind for our own animals. What a life for a child to get frightened just because she had chosen to put her own animals first. I need not have worried and my mother would have supported and defended me anyway. No, it was this. My teacher had obtained a book with outstanding extracts from German literature and a vast selection of poetry from about 1100 to 1920 and he had thought it would be just right for me. But it was to be kept secret. The Nazi regime frowned on German literature if it was not heroic and 'forward storming' and the 1940 German school text books mainly contained verses – I say verses and not poetry – by new and approved German authors. Not all of them were awful. Some songs and poems were truly sparkling gems of the German language. One of my favourites was '*Hohe Nacht der klaren Sterne*' by Nazi propagandist Hans Baumann.

I had to promise my mother not to mention this book to anyone; only a few members of my family knew. And I was not to say thank you to my teacher as proof that I could keep a secret. I kept the secret.

I loved the book, I spent every spare minute learning dozens of poems by heart. It was almost a compulsion, as if I knew how much I would need all those poems in just a few months' time to stop myself from sinking into irreversible despair.

Bombing raids were increasing in broad daylight. We often counted formations of more than 100 overhead, and before one formation was out of sight another followed, then more and more. The air was reverberating with the low, droning sounds. We children ran outside dancing about in the gardens and fields competing with one another as to who could count the fastest. And we counted hundreds. Air raid sirens were so commonplace that we took it as a signal to play bombers, rushing about with arms outspread in circles and figures of eight. We thought this was great fun. Oh, how we were cheated out of our childhood.

We did have a state-of-the-art air raid shelter underground, which my family built following the instructions of one of my uncles, who learned this skill when serving in Russia. The Russians were masters in building underground shelters and hideaways in double-quick time. Ours was solidly built out of huge tree trunks and packed with sandbags with the 'living quarters' at right angles away from the entrance, so you were quite well protected from the blast of an explosion. Unless the bunker took a direct hit, which was unlikely, we were quite safe. We soon learned the direction the bombers were coming from and the flight path they took. We knew which town they had unloaded their bombs on, judging by the time it took them to return. Returning bombers have a different sound. Sad really that this kind of knowledge was added to my repertoire of how to be aware and beware of the ways of the world. The bombers became the bane of my life. They were a constant reminder of the uncertainty of one's lifespan, which could end in a flash. Today, tomorrow? Perhaps there were only minutes of precious life left. There was a constant, nagging fear overshadowing your every step. Waking up in the morning was the beginning of a nightmarish day. And that was not all. These gleaming silvery bombers dropped thousands and thousands of gleaming silvery strips. How they sparkled and danced in the sunlight and settled in the yard, in the garden, in the fields. No resemblance to Grimm's fairy tale about the little girl and the *Sterntaler* (*The Star Talers,* in which a little girl gives away everything she has, to be rewarded with silver 'pennies' from heaven). In the fairy tale the silver falling from the sky was sheer joy and a just reward for being a good girl. I was also a good girl. But I received only frustration, hunger and hard work for being so. This kind of silver did not fall from heaven and had to be collected and handed in at our headquarters. It was forbidden to leave the silver strips lying on the land. Wardens went round inspecting the fields. There was no way out and I felt increasingly angry as more and more of my life was stolen and what life was left to me became blighted.

Still it got worse; in the form of the lovely Colorado beetles. School lessons were cancelled. Instead we were marched out into nearby villages and groups of us were assigned a certain number of acres of potato fields. It was back-breaking, energy-intensive work. The fields were often waterlogged, as they had not been properly ploughed and drained for some time, our shoes got stuck in the mud, our clothes were often drenched by rain. We were totally exhausted and cold, having walked miles and miles in a day looking for the beetles hiding on the undersides of the leaves. The harvest was lots and lots of these pretty beetles floating dead in our tins and jars half filled with water. When I got home, having helped clear other people's fields, I could make a start on our own potato fields. The only thought that kept me – and, I am sure, all the others – going was the certainty that without our superhuman efforts there would be even less to eat in autumn and winter. Hamsters have exercise wheels; we, children and grown-ups alike, had treadmills and if you faltered and stopped your lot would be death by starvation and exhaustion for sure.

The final insult was this: at our BDM meetings the names of those who had collected the most beetles were read out like a roll of honour. I was livid. My name was never mentioned. It was not my fault that these ghastly planes had not dropped more beetles on my patch. How I loathed these bombers and all the other planes, whatever make they were, I would have shot all of them down if only I could have done so, regardless of what they dropped, bombs, beetles or silver strips. They made my life a misery. Of course it was not only my life that was no longer worth living. I shared this fate with millions of others.

In later years I thought, why silver strips? Why not information leaflets? If the Allied forces knew details about the wicked and psychopathic actions that Hitler & Co took against Jews and other non-Aryans, why not let us know, tell us where and when these crimes were committed? There was a lot of unrest in the country already. The First World War for Germany had never finished. People were still trying to find their feet when Hitler came to power with a minority vote. It must have been a staggering coup. After the Versailles Treaty, with its unrealistic reparations, most properties were so over-taxed that most of ours had to be sold. With money raised from the sale subsequently lost in the hyper inflation, I know that what had remained of our property had to be remortgaged in 1919 just to put food on the table. It was paid off in 1939. Then my family thought, now we can make a new start.

We did. Headlong into catastrophe and death for most of us. The Nazis were masters at covering up and playing a two-faced game. My uncle's German shepherd dog one night attacked a burglar in their small animal house. Only it wasn't a burglar, as he thought. It was only a POW looking for something to eat. Unfortunately, Hasso, the dog, bit him. My uncle and aunt were very good souls and if only the POW had knocked at their front door, they would have shared what little they had to eat, as they and we had always done. My mother's words, 'Remember, all people are like us,' always ring in my ears. We don't know what happened to the POW. But an official arrived the next morning and poor Hasso was shot. The official said that a dog that attacks and bites a person, POW or not, is dangerous and his orders were to shoot him. There was no appeal to mercy or common sense.

With hindsight the Nazi regime played a despicable double game. And I would have been aghast had I known that I was by now No. 1 on the world's hit list. And that I and millions of other Germans should be killed by whatever means because we were wicked, murderous monsters. Had I known I would have been riveted to the spot with amazement, just as I had been years ago as a small person dressed in white on hearing that I was a cousin. But then, of course, I think that our enemy was not really interested in bringing the war to a premature end. There is a lot of money to be made out of making and selling arms. Why rob yourself of a profit? You may well kill mainly women and children as they are easy targets, in revenge for millions of innocents murdered, so go ahead and murder a few more million innocents. I am sure for some it is easier on their conscience doing it that way. These revenge killings have a feel-good factor about them. It makes the victors feel proud of their deeds. The English language goes right to the heart of this kind of problem with very few words: two wrongs don't make a right.

For the world to assume that all Germans were or are hateful killers is indefensible. People who think this have twisted minds themselves and I would not trust them and it would be wise to steer clear of them. In all my desperate times in 1945, when death missed me by a whisker many a time, when I was witness to unimaginable depravity, I will never forget the good, compassionate people that I had the fortune to meet. It is with great joy and thankfulness that I feel vindicated in believing that good people vastly outnumber the bad ones. When millions were so severely tested, those with compassion for their fellow human beings won hands down. There is one problem, however: a single bad man with a machine gun can kill hundreds of the good ones.

It was not only the physical hardship that wore me down, the never-ending, pointless, life-wasting hard work, the cold, the wet, the sleepless fearful nights, the lack of rest at any time of day because of bombing raids, the marching, the singing, the thirst, the hunger, the overwhelming powerlessness; the absence of hope and joy with no end in sight sapped my energy and almost destroyed my ability to day dream. I resorted to dancing whenever I could be by myself, humming some sad Nordic melodies or some other melancholic music by Chopin or Sibelius. Dancing was my wonder cure and it helped me to pick myself up again and make a fresh start. My favourite dance was *Valse Triste*.

Whenever called by my mother I hurried to her and I deliberately put on a smile. I knew she had only me, I was the only man in the house and I felt she deserved a smiling face. Once, she asked, do you ever stop smiling child? And I replied, no, because your life is harder than mine. I am now proud that I said this and I knew that I was fully aware of what I was saying. I had tried to be supportive of her and I was growing out of childhood.

To the physical burden of daily life was added the mental grief and anguish. It had been the custom that in the case of a death in a family the eldest girl was sent to the bereaved with flowers and card to convey formally the condolences of her family to the *Trauerhaus* (the house or family in mourning). Everyone at some point in their lives comes into contact with death. The formalities and customs surrounding such an event to some extent channel feelings of shock and sadness away from the immediate impact of the death of a loved one. There were many things to be observed when visiting a Trauerhaus. A child had to be clean, face and hands properly washed, hair brushed, dress neat, tidy and spotless, shoes had to shine. She must wear a quiet, calm face and approach the chief mourner in a respectful manner, curtsy, not get her words in a twist, remember to shake hands with her right, pass the flowers and card with her left and look the person receiving them in the eye. Once thanked, she must curtsy, turn and walk away with quiet dignity. Well done.

But there was a war on. And I visited virtually every house in my neighbourhood, some not just once but several times. Not only were the people who had died known to me, some had been my childhood friends, although a few years older than me. The boys were called up at age 16 to serve their country. The first house I visited to discharge my duties was that of my friend, my blonde Ingeborg; her brother Ingolf was the victim. It seemed such a short time ago that we had played cops and robbers at the edge of our forest. Now I stood before his mother with my card and flowers. She stood there so silent, so dignified, dressed in black with a pale face and reddened eyes, like all the other women that I was required to honour and respect with my visit on behalf of my family.

No one had actually given a thought to the little girl to whom the death of friends and neighbours had become a routine. And even if someone had considered my feelings, my fear and dread of every day, it would not have made any difference. My mother said she was so sad for me, but there was no one else we could send to the bereaved. That's war for you. It is cruel to all: the innocent, the guilty, the morally neutral.

At school, four girls had become my best friends, my blonde Ingeborg, my auburn Ingeborg, clever Irene and very warm-hearted, very affectionate Lizzy. I liked all of them so much, and their families. Their fathers, elder brothers and sisters had long been called up to defend the Fatherland. The fathers of Irene and blonde Ingeborg had been lucky: one was ill with something strange called diabetes and the other one was 'chesty'. They worked at the town hall giving out ration cards. In September 1944 Irene's parents gave a farewell party for their son Erwin. He had completed his emergency final school exams and had been called up to serve in the Navy. It was a happy afternoon with ersatz food and ersatz coffee and Erwin showed us some of his card tricks. I will forever remember his laughter as he bamboozled us with his quick-fingered, elegant deceptions. I visited the family again less than a fortnight later with my card, my flowers and condolence message. Erwin was now at the bottom of the sea in a U-boat, off Heligoland.

My auburn Ingeborg arrived at school late one day for lessons, she was crying. They had had a telegram, her daddy had died in the war and her mother was taking her and her sister Sigrid to Breslau to see her daddy's parents. I was so upset to see Ingeborg leaving the classroom still crying, accompanied by our teacher holding her hand and talking to her quietly. I could not say goodbye and a few days later we heard that the entire family had been wiped out during a bombing raid in Breslau. None of my four close friends, nor their families, survived the next few months. With my auburn Ingeborg, the countdown to zero had begun.

Life became an even more fearsome, insecure existence as the days passed. And yet I was the lucky one: only I and some members of my family lived beyond the early months of 1945. That says something about the death rate east of the Oder. Most perished – by violence, cold and hunger, in that order. I was there. I saw the unimaginable terror unfold. The number of dead? Approximately? Think of a high number and add noughts to it. You will still underestimate. No one who was not actually on the roads in Germany east of the Oder during the first few months of 1945 has the imagination required even remotely to conjure up the reality.

For now, I am still in October 1944. My last birthday party is at home with now only one Ingeborg, one Irene and one Lizzy. We lived it up with 'coffee' made from acorns, *Zichorie*, dandelion root and, oh, extravagance, some barley. We burnt the *Kaffe* ourselves (with only one 'e' – real *Kaffee* made from coffee beans has two). No candles, of course, they were strictly for black-out lighting, but we had cake made from boiled mashed potatoes, ersatz margarine and marzipan essence. What a wicked feast. My little brothers were at the table singing my birthday song with gusto, and my dainty, delicate little sister with her silver hair and her huge blue-grey eyes. My little sister was unusually clever, with such an inventive, lively imagination. She left us way behind. She could make up the most interesting stories and could tell them with such conviction that her fantastic tales seemed quite real and utterly believable. Wherever she went there was always a crowd of children begging her to tell a story. There was no end to her kindness, willingness and the ease with which she could think up another story. Not only I, but all grown-ups found her talent quite exquisite and extraordinary.

FOOD, ALWAYS FOOD

Autumn 1944 became a truly anxious time, above all because of the food shortage. Life revolved around potatoes. Risk digging them up early, when the yield was still quite small, when they were not ripe and would therefore not store well; or leave them in the ground in the field to find that they had been dug up during the night by somebody or several bodies, who were smart and equally hungry. Either way that would decrease your yield. My mother just sighed. There was no longer a right way of doing things. Roads and railways were destroyed in bombing raids, what little food there was could not be distributed and if a food transport was on the way somebody would know about it and it was intercepted, meaning ambushed and stolen.

There were no longer beechnuts on beeches, no acorns on oaks, no chestnuts on chestnut trees, no wild apples, no pears, no berries, no plantains, no nettles, no rose hips. Where had it all gone? Presumably into large bags like the one that I had always tied round my waist, filling it with whatever came my way to be taken back home triumphantly. We behaved, at least I did, like squirrels. Finding and hiding food was task number one. It meant you had food when others had none. You could share it if your conscience did not allow you to hog it all. With food you were in a strong position. Even if in fact you had more than you could eat yourself. With extras stashed away you could barter. With food you had a distinct advantage over your fellow human beings who were without.

My auntie who had held the secret dinner parties in her kitchen had access to sugar, which in turn she swapped for glass jars and bottles to preserve food in. She used to ask me quite often to see her at such and such a time to take away bottles and jars full of preserves and told me to 'dig them in somewhere safe and make sure no one sees you doing it.' This I did. Often I had no time to tell my mother first what I was digging in, how much, where and when. The area around our bomb shelter in particular was soon pitted with jars of plums, apples, pears, even rhubarb, normally only used in spring. Nothing was left growing above ground. I dug in carrots, yellow fodder carrots for rabbits, swedes, potatoes, apple puree in bottles, stacks of walnuts, hazelnuts, even pots with lard covered with straw first and then with sand. My town was built on what was called *Märkischer Sand*, the end product of a *Moräne* (an accumulation of glacial debris) after the ice age. It made a clean, efficient, porous storage cellar for food. Thinking back, actually only I knew where all of it was hidden. It turned out to be just as well.

That autumn in 1944 brought so much upheaval that I don't know where to start. The bombing raids became so frequent that it was virtually impossible to go to school. We were tired constantly and made our way to and from school from bomb shelter to bomb shelter. At whichever point you were on your way to town you had to know where your nearest shelter was. Where will you run to if the siren goes when you are in such and such a street? You better know the answer to that or you could be gone. My mother eventually stopped me going to school; that was after Christmas 1944. She considered the bomb shelters in town too unsafe, as they were usually in cellars which were no protection if the house on top of you collapsed or caught fire, or the water pipes burst and drowned you.

And then there was the flood of refugees. Day after day women arrived on our door step with children and elderly or sick relatives in tow. The story was always the same. 'Good woman, we have walked for weeks to get away from Zhukow's army, we can walk no further, let us in.' And in they came. My mother slept with my sister and my two brothers in one bed, two at the top and two at the bottom end of the bed. I was dispatched to my grandparents' wing where I occupied a kind of makeshift bed in a store room next to the larder, which had a secret door to one of the cellars. The rest of the house was given up to refugees. My room was no longer my room, my clothes not my clothes, they belonged to whoever they fitted and my toys were not my toys. I just hid my favourite Käthe Kruse doll. I did not mind sharing my books.

The refugees kept coming. The amazing thing was how many of them did not speak a word of German. Our Polish POWs often did the translating. The refugees came from Poland, Belarus, the Ukraine and places so far away they might have been on another planet. My mother just waved them into the house. 'But there are no beds left and very little food.' It didn't matter; they slept on the floor, sat on the stairs, slept on the landing, crowded the upper floors, stayed in the attics, crammed into the loft and some even stayed in great-grandfather's cellar, which had no windows and only ventilation shafts. Great-grandfather slept in the barn with some of our POWs to guard the rabbits. The POWs were very loyal. Our POWs had by now become family, they stayed with all of us inside the house and certainly did not want to go back to camp. My mother asked if they did not get into trouble with the guards for not going back and staying later and later and in the end not going back at all. Oh no, they said, the guards are not there either. They have all gone AWOL. Of course, how silly not to think of it. A camp without warmth, light or food has nothing for guards or inmates and everyone had made their own arrangements.

Our Polish POWs seemed to be more fearful for some reason because of the Russian advance. I did not know why but a few weeks later the answer became clear. The French POWs were more forthcoming, more talkative and, although this seems quite frivolous to say, very entertaining. The German radio stations were of course jammed by the Nazi regime, meaning you could not get any news other than what was permitted. But our French POWs had cobbled together home-made radios and the news they relayed to us was so different from the German news that both versions seemed unbelievable. As it turned out later, much later and too late for us, the French news was closer to reality than the German news.

Food, or the absence of it, became a preoccupation for everyone. If you thought three potatoes per person per day and nothing else was a miserable diet, then you were clearly deluded. New recipes to make a potato go further were invented by us every day. We had Eureka moments. Boil water, a fair bit of it, say one litre, then take one smallish potato with peel, grate it into the boiling water and the water will turn into a slimy greenish transparent soup. The grated potato thickens the water. Take more, say five potatoes, and lots more water, until you have enough 'soup' to go round for a large number of people. If you don't have enough potatoes to make more soup, then just add more water. If only we could have had a pinch of salt with it. The lack of salt was quite maddening. We had already used up the orange-coloured salt used as licking stones for cattle. Well, there was no more and that was that. All good things must come to an end.

It did get worse. I keep saying this, but it was really true. One day uniformed people arrived and arrested my mother. We were almost paralysed with shock and fear. What on earth had happened? It was this. Sweets had been called up on the ration cards. Only a few grams but, nonetheless, most valuable food. The news spread like wildfire and like others, my mother had rushed to the local shop where they were distributed. There she heard that the sweets were for Aryan children only. Whereupon my dearest mother uttered the ominous words which almost cost us our lives. 'But why? All children like sweets.'You cannot utter such heinous words with a Hitler in power. Later on my mother recalled that she was in such shock and confusion that she could no longer remember who was in the shop when she had made this unpatriotic remark. It is also possible that someone equally innocently told someone else, who then denounced my mother. She was held for three days to explain her attitude to Hitler. But her brother, who had long since been listed as missing and unbeknown to us had been held as a POW in North Africa before being shipped to California to work in a cotton plantation, was a hero. He had, under heavy bombing and enemy fire, saved a lot of people from a burning, collapsing hospital building, risking his own life. He had explained later to us that it did not really matter what he did. The burning building was on the point of collapse. 'I could either go in and drag people out while I could still move and be killed by the burning building or I could have stayed outside and be killed by the ferocious gun fire and exploding shells. What would you have done?' After the battle had subsided he even managed to carry some of the more seriously wounded to a plane that flew them out of the battle zone. He himself refused to take up a place on the plane and stayed behind at his post. He had some toes amputated later; they had got a bit fried. Later still, he had some more bits of toe amputated, this time having been frozen off in the Russian winter. Anyway, his bravery had been reported by the wounded and my uncle was awarded the Iron Cross, First Class. Little did he know that by rescuing vulnerable strangers he had also rescued his sister and her family. The SS decided we were not such a bad family after all. They let my mother go.

Once my uncle told us how he got lost on his own as a dispatch rider; in Russia, in winter, at night. He found an army unit several hundred strong huddled round some fires and assumed they were German. When he entered the encampment he found they were not. But the night was cold and not one of the Russian soldiers bothered to get up from under their great coats. They just looked at him. Shoot? Why? Russia is big and the winter is cold. He found a *datschka* (a simple house) later. A woman there looked after him until the next morning and gave him a crust of bread as a farewell. He said that he had felt very tearful and maybe this kind woman thought perhaps someone, somewhere, would help her son in the same way. In all good conscience I can answer 'Mütterchen Rußland, we did.'

When my mother arrived back home she was shaken, visibly thinner and seething with barely contained fury about her treatment. Alas, one could not fight back. Our POWs were also clearly relieved, not only because they genuinely liked my mother but also because her release probably saved their lives. If my mother had been found guilty of subversive actions by quite openly opposing Hitler's ideologies she would have been shot and everyone related to her, or only vaguely connected, would have suffered the same fate, as collaborators.

I may have been a child but the horrendous and bizarre challenge to my understanding of good and evil struck me like lightning. I became fully aware that all of us were mere pawns in the clutches of some great evil that we could not fight and that we had no control over. We were helpless. 'Do your work promptly, quietly, attract no attention, listen, observe, be vigilant and above all keep your mouth shut, but report back to me everything you hear and see without fail.' These were the instructions of my mother to me. They were taken seriously and obeyed. I had learned enough to know that the tiniest deviation from what was regarded as normal behaviour or routine could bring an abrupt end to your existence. Any misdemeanour would drag other innocents around you into a hellish trap from which there was no return. We had to be most careful not to be seen speaking to our POWs, they clearly understood the implications and equally tried their hardest to pretend that we did not exist. And yet we had to work together. It was like invisible ghosts speaking to other invisible ghosts. A mockery was made of life. Our regulars still kept coming back at night, long whispered conversations were held, no longer by the light of a candle. Candles? They were a memory. We burnt small strips of linen, one strip at a time of course, in a small dish containing lard or other fat if we had some. It was a dim, smoky type of light with dark oily threads floating up into the air, and as you would expect it smelt revolting.

Every so often the linen strip would slip back into the dish and we were shrouded in darkness. You might think just strike another match and light the strip again. Where would you find the match? They were no longer for sale. A fire was precious.

Fires were guarded in the kitchen stove and never allowed to go out. If you had that misfortune then you had to go and beg fire from a neighbour. We had extremely convenient fire vessels from the olden days still in the loft, in the form of old-fashioned irons. They had the shape of modern irons but had a heavy double base with holes along both sides of the base. You needed the holes so that air could get to the glowing embers with which the base was filled. We never had to collect fire, we always had several on the go, as you would expect in a large house. People who had to come from some distance away to our place for a light used to cover the irons with bits of old horse blanket, as these were tough enough not to catch fire quickly and they cut down on the air flowing through the holes. The faster you walked with your fire, the brighter it would glow as more air flowed through the holes. If you were not careful with the embers, then they would be cold when you arrived with them at your own house, which could be far away.

My mother never turned a blind eye to other people's needs, in spite of the fact that she had to be obsessively careful after her arrest. One day, five POWs we had never seen before and looking very poorly knocked on our door begging for food, obviously needing it. We had at the time the most meagre rations for ourselves. But my mother had baked a loaf; it was a large loaf, perhaps a six-pounder containing a fair share of potatoes. I know it was not good bread because I had been sent with a large jug to the barn to get some of the rabbits' bran. It was more husk than bran. My mother asked me to fetch the bread. And then a lengthy palaver started, I could not make out in which languages. The discussion was about one loaf, five big men and nine smallish children. Although the men were larger by bulk than all the children put together, it was agreed that the children needed more of the bread. So in the end, everyone was in agreement that a fair share was the larger portion for the children, a smaller 'half' for the five men. The bread was cut accordingly there and then on the doorstep. My mother could, of course, have said to them, 'No, we have no food to share.' But she never did such a heartless thing to anyone. We took life as it presented itself day by day and hour by hour. One minute you could think you were alright, you had secured your food for a couple of days, the next minute your plans were overthrown and you had to adjust to a completely new and unforeseen situation. But we were satisfied that there and then the correct decision had been made; and I was learning while clinging to her apron strings. Life was a daily struggle. Tomorrow, yes, tomorrow you would have to rethink your strategy for survival.

Well, tomorrow brought an unexpected surprise. The five men turned up again and with big smiles handed my mother a basket, just completed, woven out of still wet willow roots as their big thank you and appreciation for the excuse of a loaf the day before. My mother was very touched and almost cried. She was proved right again: *all people are like you and me* ... The basket was hidden like treasure to show my father when he came back from the war. Although he was presumed dead at El Alamein, my mother refused even to consider such a possibility.

In mid-January 1945 our POWs implored us most urgently to leave and go west. Zhukow's army was getting close and they felt if they were overtaken by the Russian army they would be safer with them than we would be. How mistaken they were. According to German news reports the Russian army was well to the east of us and not even in Posen, and should they get near Landsberg or thereabouts there would still be time for us to leave safely for the western side of the Oder. How mistaken *we* were.

Of course, we had a plan. Close relatives lived in Kalenzig, a village bordering the Oder with land on both sides of the river. A ferry with a hand-operated mechanism would get you back and forth. The ferry was large enough to take horses with a hay wagon but then it took two men to operate the mechanism. I had spent quite a few holidays with our relatives and adored crossing the river. If you were late back in the evening and the ferry was already on the other side then there were rowing boats you could use to paddle yourself back home. I loved every minute of it. So, if it should come to it that we had to leave home, we would go to Uncle Karl and Auntie Minna and we would cross the Oder from there. They would wait for us and with the river by the front gate we could not fail to get across to relative safety; which meant running as far and as fast as you could until you reached the British Army, which was expected to be somewhere in the north-west of Germany. Wrong again.

BIDDING FAREWELL
TO GRANDFATHER

There was another influx of refugees. Our house was now so full that newcomers did not even know who the owners were, nor did it matter. There was a roof over our heads, it was warm and dry. Air raids were ignored, it was cold outside, potentially more dangerous to underfed people than the chance of a direct hit. If fate had it in for you then there was nothing you could do about it. But it was very distressing to listen to all these accounts of lost or dead relatives, lost children, lost mothers, and with no way of knowing what had happened to them, no means of finding out anything about their fate. Why did so many of them not speak or understand a word of German? I gathered this much as a child: if the words 'Marshal Zhukow' are uttered, run for it. I lived in a dangerous and complicated world.

My mother decided that we children had to learn basic survival techniques, how to behave and what to do should we have to join the stream of refugees ahead of the Russian army. 'Very important, if we get separated don't just shout "mummy, mummy". All children do that. Shout "mummy Wendy Jones" or "mummy Richard Smith". Mummy must be given a name.' We had to practise shouting at the top of our voices, calling about half a dozen times, then rest, don't panic and start shouting again. We had to learn our full names, date and place of birth, name of town, name of street, house name or number, in the district of … In our case: Kreis Königsberg, Neumark. Neumark was important as opposed to Kreis Königsberg, Ostpreußen. We had to rehearse this several times a day. Remember the names of your brothers and sisters. Even my youngest brother had to learn it. Not only that, we were labelled according to the wise old saying: my vest is closer to me than my pants. Our vests were embroidered with our now very lengthy names. And we wore two or three vests each, not only because it was bitterly cold in the winter of 1944/45 but also because washing and drying clothes had become virtually impossible under the onslaught of so many people in our house. And it was best to be warmly dressed at all times, in case we had to leave suddenly.

One day towards the end of January 1945 our POWs gave us their last warning. The Russians would arrive any day according to their news, not, of course, to German news. So, there we were; we had reached the end of the road we had travelled together for so long. Thanks again for everything, look after yourself, keep your beak up, all the best, we are off. We were very upset when they left; we had known some of them for several years. The French were somewhat relieved. They travelled west, away from the Russian army. Our Polish POWs were fearful. They knew more about the Russian war machine than we did and they knew why all of us should fear it. Some stayed in hiding, two stayed with us. One French POW stayed in hiding, he was engaged to one of my mother's cousins, a horrendously dangerous situation for both of them. It had been kept ever so secret. So our house emptied. Everyone ran west to get across the Oder.

Later we learned that they were doomed. The Russian army had not been interested in our area. They were off to Peenemünde. The V2 rockets were launched from there. Another section of their army went right through to Berlin, the old and well-trodden route Moskau, Warschau, Küstrin, Berlin. Küstrin had been a heavily fortified town for hundreds of years, the fortifications reinforced by Frederick the Great. So why stop and fight for Küstrin? They bypassed the town and crossed north of it, near Schwedt. And then they came back at us from the west. The poor people who had left our place had run straight into the crossfire along the east side of the Oder; their chances of survival had been next to nil. They were also hit by another piece of ill fortune because there were vast numbers of soldiers from the east of the Urals, many from the Mongolian steppes and so far away from Europe that France, Poland, Germany or any country in western Europe was beyond their experience and they had no concept of western languages. All they knew was that these people did not look like them, did not speak like them, they were in enemy country and if it moved it had to be killed. Which is what they did.

To be, through good luck, in an area with relatively little fighting contributed to our initial survival. We, the survivors, were in the minority. Most people met a violent death. Countless thousands perished with no one left to tell the tale. But some lived. I lived and I find it extremely hard to pass on the unfolding, relentless, horror that engulfed us in the east in January 1945.

Germany also had its Dad's Army – the *Volkssturm*. They had no power; they could not defend anyone, not even themselves. Even the youngest, under 16 years of age, the very old, the disabled, no matter how unfit, were called up, sacrificed, slaughtered senselessly in the name of I don't know what, and nobody else knew either. If you hesitated or disobeyed you were shot as a traitor or coward or whatever sprang to mind. It was best to go along with events and hope something would happen to save your life, if not you were dead there and then and your family with you.

It was 31 January 1945. One of the few dates I remember exactly, when war became a reality for us. I slept in the very small room next to the secret cellar. This room had been kept by my grandparents for themselves and for me. Most of the house was still full of refugees.

As others had departed, new ones filled the empty spaces, just for a rest, then they would go and other exhausted unfortunates would take their place. I remember no squabbles, no loud words, just despair, silence and tears. As I slept in my grandmother's bed in that tiny room there was a knock at the window at about 4am. Not loud, just enough to wake us up. The shutters muffled the sound. It was an icy night. My grandfather quietly opened the front door. Two uniformed men came in and into my grandparent's kitchen. They whispered. The Russians are approaching. Get yourself ready quickly, come with us. You and others will be taken to Küstrin to defend the Fatherland.

While I stood frightened in my nightie in the kitchen, my grandfather got dressed, my grandmother hurriedly got together a bundle of warm clothes and some food and within minutes I was hugged and kissed goodbye; don't make a noise, don't cry, let the others and mummy have their sleep, be a good, brave girl, I will be back as soon as I can. The front door closed, the light flickered and I could hear steps moving away across the frozen snow outside. I stood there unmoving. I did not know what to do with my grandmother. She had slumped into a chair with her head resting on the table.

Nothing seemed to happen for an eternity and then, suddenly, my grandmother began to cry and I just stood there. I had never seen my grandmother cry, always so composed, so practical, always knowing what to do and now she needed help. She had come through the First World War, the distress of a wounded then crippled husband, the inflation, the hunger, the flu epidemic (she lost a child to the flu in 1919), the struggle to survive and keep the property and clear a crippling mortgage thereafter. Then two sons and one son-in-law were missing in action in this war and now her elderly husband was taken away; of course she cried. Not knowing how to help her, I started moving towards the kitchen door to get my mother, although I had been told to let her sleep as it was so early. I collided with my mother at the door as I opened it. The loud crying had awakened her and she had rushed from her rooms to my grandparents' part of the house. She was clearly shocked when told what had happened. Great-grandfather and other members of the family now also crowded into the kitchen.

'So, father went away without saying goodbye? I will not let him go without a farewell,' my mother said. 'I will take the first train to Küstrin and find him, and you,' she said, turning to me, 'get dressed warmly, you will come with me. We will be out all day.' Being the eldest and official future owner of the property, it was my important duty to represent all other grandchildren and bid my grandfather a proper farewell as was due to him on their behalf. I nodded and got myself ready, fit enough to go to the North Pole – which was just as well. Our relatives attended to all the other children, my mother packed a few things, among them a gas fire lighter and some precious fire stones, and off we went, still in the dark, to the station to catch a train.

Timetables meant nothing any more. A train would come if it got through. It might not come at all. There were no other civilians, only uniformed people at the station, looking like us – cold, hungry, frozen, faces grey with stress. Daylight came, morning came, midday came, no train. Aircraft overhead, not German ones, all enemy planes; who cared, they were so commonplace. So what? We were all bomb happy. Then at last around 14.00 hours the sound of a train. Not a train as you picture in your mind, with windows all round, steps leading up to a carriage, upholstered seats. Such trains had long since disappeared. There were only goods trains now, and they were very long. The locomotive worked very hard and the train made only slow progress and was a wonderful target for hostile fire, a most desirable morsel for fighter planes.

We did not know then that we would be on the very last train from the east in the direction of Küstrin–Berlin. The train had been attacked by enemy planes, the bombs had missed but the track east of and close to my town had been destroyed. So, no more trains. The soldiers tried to help us find a space for two on the goods wagons. They opened a few wagons – the wagons could only be opened from outside – they seemed to know what was inside them. Virtually all remained closed, then there was a voice from one wagon, alright in here for two, the soldiers hurried us along. I was lifted high up, passed from one pair of arms to another and then deposited on top of a box with little space between that and the roof of the wagon. My mother was lifted in as well, the doors closed with a bang, the train started moving and we cowered in our dark little prison cell. That is what it seemed to be. 'Are you alright up there?' asked a voice. 'Make yourself comfy.'

Knowing that my mother was there as well, I assured the darkness politely that I was fine. Actually I was not. I seemed to be sitting on a box full of knobbly potatoes with only a thin layer of sacking on top. It was, in fact, jolly uncomfortable. Then someone struck a match and lit a candle. Now we could see our company: soldiers' faces materialised out of the gloom, crammed between tightly stacked boxes, hardly any room to move, all gathered around a box on which the candle had been stuck. The soldiers continued with a card game, my mother was invited to join in and there we were, apart from me, all playing cards, accompanied by light-hearted banter, some jokes, laughter. War? What about it? Wasn't everyone passing their time like we did? Had there ever been another world? Must have been a long time ago, before our time, anyway.

The soldiers declared my mother mad to try to find her father in Küstrin amid the general chaos and upheaval and she, in turn, declared the entire war mad and everyone in it, so being mad was the norm. The train moved on very slowly indeed, it seemed to be stationary most of the time. We knew there was extensive forest between my town and Küstrin and it was noticeable that the train stopped when there was the sound of enemy planes in the air. We were finely tuned to the sound of planes, bombers or fighter planes, and we knew who was who. It was obvious that our little train was hiding under the canopy of trees along the line to Küstrin and only moving when the air was clear.

Once in the middle of the droning of enemy planes my mother said 'Who will look for us if we get hit?' *Weinen Sie nicht, schöne, junge Frau.* Don't cry, pretty young woman. No one will look for us if we take a hit. We carry ammunition, said a voice with a very reassuring tone.

Good-natured laughter from the other soldiers. It sounded as if they had finished with their lives. They were taking what was handed out to them philosophically. No one had the power to change their fate. I knew I was not sitting on potatoes, but on hand grenades with that well known pattern by now well imprinted on my bottom. The calm with which these soldiers accepted their fate made me one of them. But my heart beat a lot faster every time another formation of enemy planes sounded overhead.

The short journey of about 17km took about five hours. When we arrived at Küstrin it was obviously pitch dark. The soldiers passed us to some officer with a vehicle. He listened sympathetically and, declaring my mother mad again, passed us to another group of officers who seemed to be in the know and they took us by army truck to barracks reserved for *Volkssturm* recruits. And so good was their organisation that the officer in charge in the guardroom confirmed that they had a person with such a name in rooms numbered xyz. He listened with astonishment to my mother's reason for her journey to say goodbye to her father. He immediately sent orders to fetch my grandfather from his room and organised a visit to the toilets for us as theirs were for men only. I thought it was very grand as I had never before visited a toilet accompanied by a soldier with a rifle. One had one's moments.

Back in the guard room my grandfather arrived with a big smile on his face. 'I knew you would come,' he said and held out a gigantic salami which he had swapped for a jumper from one of his new comrades, who had taken plenty of food but not enough warm clothing. Uniforms had not been issued. There weren't any. We exchanged hugs and kisses, constantly implored by the officer to stay at the barracks, which would be safe for us. There were no more trains going east, in fact, there was no more transport of any kind going east because of possible infiltration by the enemy. I am sure, with hindsight, he knew more than that, hence his desperate attempts to keep us at his barracks. My mother was undeterred. She knew the area from childhood like the back of her hand and would find her way back home without using the main road.

So, after a final hug and a confident, encouraging nod from my grandfather, we left in the pitch dark and ventured into the icy world of winter in the east, heading east where my mother's other children were waiting. It was tough going. There had been plenty of snow, which gave the forest a ghostly appearance. Here and there we heard a rustle in the bushes, we thought we could hear voices, we stopped and all was silent again. I felt like screaming with fear, my mother whispered keep quiet, very, very quiet, hold my hand and keep walking, look down, don't look around. After a few kilometres a dark figure came out of the bushes, a German soldier. 'Stop, good woman,' he said in a hushed voice, 'don't go further, come back with me. It is unsafe in the direction you are going.' 'I have to go on, my children are in that town.' This happened four or five times, then no more.

Another few kilometres on we thought again we could hear whispering and rustling noises, but no one came forward any more. Later we knew they had been Russian soldiers, possibly equally puzzled to see a woman with a child passing that way. There was clearly no point in giving their positions away because of us. We were actually quite safe; we were passing through enemy-held land and the enemy did not want anyone to know that they were there. But it was eerie, and the walk in thick snow higher than my knees began to take its toll. I was exhausted, cold, I could have fallen flat on my face and died, I would not have cared. By a road sign we passed I knew that we were still more than ten kilometres away from home and warmth, safety, food and sleep. We came to a junction with a house to the right; I wished we could stop, knock at the door and ask to stay for a rest, but my mother's hand pulled me forward, whether I walked under my own steam or whether she dragged me on, we were making for home, it was of overriding importance, no ifs and no buts, we had to get home.

The road sign, barely visible above the height of the snow, displayed the name of my town. I will remember this forever. At that point I started to cry. I cried silently, battling with my exhaustion, not knowing whether I would have the strength to pull through, they were the hottest tears I ever shed. I did not know how strong I would have to be and whether I would be able to live up to my own demands.

About fifty years later I saw a photo of that spot in a Polish paper. The house was still there. The road sign now showed the Polish word for my town. The photo provoked a pang of anguish within me. But it was merely the outer symbol of a deep feeling of heartbreak and injustice foisted upon ordinary people who were thrown into this cauldron of human failings; it encapsulated so much suffering and so many deaths of innocents that my mind, at least, cannot ever come to terms with it. It is beyond my comprehension.

There are now Poles living in my home, which they consider their home, my land is now their land and so many years have gone by that those who live there now have never known it to be different. Do I dislike or hate the Poles? No. Why? Should I? This turn of events was no more their fault than it was mine, nor was it the fault of my family and their doing. The Poles, like us, had been pawns of evil men at a time in history when millions had been robbed of any respect for humanity and we were thrown into a cesspit of degradation and total disregard for the wonder of life. But, still, this photo does hurt. It was my homeland. It was my family, my friends that had to die, so that they could now live there.

My mother was also battling with the cold and the height of the snow and the creepy feeling that eyes were watching us. Noises too faint to be properly identified seemed to surround us. Sometimes there was a sharp click but so unlike a snapped branch that we knew it was something sinister. And yet we stumbled on unhindered. My mother knew I was crying, although I had tried to keep it secret and she whispered that we would stop at the next village and ask someone for a hot drink before walking on. Many had knocked at our door during the past year for help, now it was our turn to knock and ask for assistance. But because of the ghostly noises that had accompanied us for quite a few kilometres, we quietly crept along garden hedges to the centre of the village.

The village had actually become quite famous about 200 years ago when Frederick the Great fought one of his battles against the

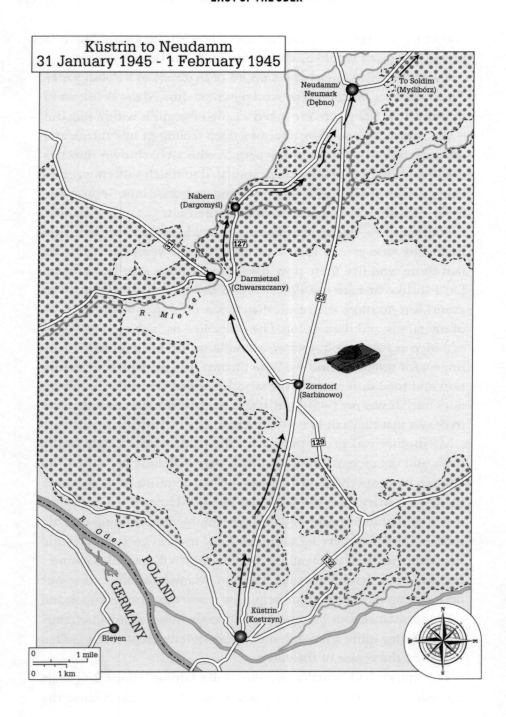

Küstrin to Neudamm
31 January 1945 - 1 February 1945

Russians there, a famous battle which he won. Our property was somehow connected with it, my grandfather knew the details. I had heard him talk about it occasionally but I can no longer get the facts in the right order. I should have paid more attention. The name of the village was Zorndorf. The last time a Russian army had reached so far west was in 1759, when they were defeated by the famous Prussian king.

And it was in Zorndorf that we saw it for the first time. My heart stopped and I was gripped by a terrible fear. There on the village green, illuminated by the white reflection of the snow, stood a monster, its gigantic silhouette black against the night sky: the Joseph Stalin II. I was virtually paralysed by terror. Its mere presence signalled abandonment of all hope. You cannot fight this. My mother put her hand over my face. There was no need. I could not have screamed if I had wanted to. The Soviet tank made our situation all too clear. You have lost.

Now in even greater distress and without the hot drink I was promised I was dragged on in the direction of my town. I tried to help by moving my ice cold, numb legs forward as best as I could. I could not stop crying, I cried silently and by now without tears. The snow was getting higher, it actually snowed and we were becoming invisible with the snow settling on our clothes. I fainted a few times. 'Walk on, child, walk on, we will soon be home.' It was not soon because we had left the main road from Zorndorf onwards and I would not attempt to guess how many kilometres that may have added to our walk from Küstrin to reach our house that night. This walk through the snow and darkness was nothing compared with what was to come.

I think I have to clarify the events of that night. We may have been the last two people to come from Küstrin to my home town. The German army was scattered on the outskirts of the town and in the surrounding woodland, I guess now within five kilometres of Küstrin. On the outer circle of the five kilometres we were approached by German soldiers hurriedly trying to persuade us to turn back or at least stay with them for safety. Then for a few kilometres we were not approached by anyone. The rustles, the clicks and hushed voices we heard then must have been the Russian army. We were saved by the fact that neither of the two armies knew exactly where the other was in that area. Any loud noises or a gunshot would have given their positions away. So they all remained in hiding, letting us pass unhindered. We were worth nothing in their deadly game.

I was later told that I could not have seen this particular Russian tank because Russian tanks were whitewashed, camouflaged, and the ISII ('I' for Iosef) had not been seen before that date in the area. But I stand by what I saw that night: a totally black silhouette against the night sky, contrasting with the glistening whiteness of the frozen snow on the ground. I identified the shape years later unerringly from photos. I can only assume, with hindsight, that it was not camouflaged because the Russian advance was so rapid in that area that there was no opportunity or need for camouflage. There was no one there to stop them, so why bother? Küstrin had such a concentration of defenders that it would have been mindless to attack the fortress. The Russian army bypassed Küstrin; just as the German army did not take on the ISIIs. The immense problem was that the Russians had more than a dozen ISIIs.

To cut the agony of that historic night short, we made it home. It had taken us only 13 hours because my mother had moved like a woman possessed. A person without children to have to get back to would never have made it through those conditions in such a short time. Even now, I cannot comprehend how I ever managed to struggle through this ordeal as a child, which was an endurance march for a grown-up.

Back to the morning of 1 February 1945. We probably arrived between nine and ten o'clock. We had already heard from a distance an unusual rumbling noise, like a distant thunder except that the noise did not stop. We also thought we could see palls of smoke over our town, but were not sure because of falling snow. How relieved everyone was when we stumbled into the yard. They had all been so worried about us; and doubly so because to our great surprise, on the day when we had left for Küstrin, Aunt Minna and Uncle Karl and their family had arrived. Although they lived on the bank of the Oder they could not get across. The Russians were already on the other side. So they ran to us, instead of, as we had planned, we to them. That was a blow. Our escape route had been cut off.

One of my aunties said she would take a bike and ride to town and find out what was going on. Perhaps there was even some food for sale somewhere. She came back within a few minutes. 'The Russians are there,' she shouted. 'The noise is from the tanks coming by the hundred from the road leading from Soldin to Küstrin. And the town is burning.' That electrified everyone. Normal routine was instantly suspended. Stay calm, put on warm, dry clothes and give me a hand, were my mother's orders. There would be no rest, no sleep. Grandmother made hot drinks, some refugees left our home hurriedly against the urgent advice of my mother. 'Even if the Russians are here you are safer inside the house than outside, the cold is bitter. Unless they shoot you, you will live longer inside than outside.' Few listened. Panic had set in by the mere mention of the Russian army.

MOTHER COURAGE

Then my mother's plan was put into action. All German flags in the house to be burnt, fast. Hitler's photo to be taken off the walls to be burnt, glass to be disposed of. *Mein Kampf*, too bulky to burn quickly, to be wrapped in my BDM uniform and buried in a shed with logs on top. All photos of my father and uncles in uniform to be wrapped and buried. Fast, faster, chop chop, get it done by yesterday. My younger siblings and cousins were left under the supervision of my grandmother. Great-grandfather dug the holes for *Mein Kampf*, several deep ones, since everyone in the household had one. The book had arrived amid controversial circumstances causing trouble when it had turned up, now it disappeared in the middle of mayhem. We were getting on top of the jobs and I was feeling something like being intoxicated by some drug. I felt unreal, floating on air instead of walking, perhaps I was hallucinating. I was certainly not myself, and yet, this was no dream, this was real, harsh, unforgiving.

Suddenly, in the middle of all that hustle and bustle, the first two Russian soldiers burst through the door, with weapons at the ready pointed at us. They shouted something in Russian we didn't understand. I felt suddenly very calm, ice cold; be calm, control every move, on an alert level from one to ten I was on ten. And what did my mother do? I did not trust my eyes. She rushed forward, pushed the weapons out of the way, she hung herself round the neck of one of the soldiers, kissed him, hugged him and then the other with exclamations of joy. She got both of them seated in two large armchairs, quickly found the last half bottle of brandy and she poured them drinks. My mother talked excitedly about her joy to be freed from Hitler, Himmler and whoever (that was the only thing that was not a lie). She sat on their laps and carried on talking a load of codswallop. They did not understand her, she did not understand them. It did not matter, each was highly delighted to meet the other. Inwardly I gasped with admiration. The soldiers, at first surprised, then animated, then convinced by my mother's friendly demeanour towards Russia in general and them in particular, laughed and patted me on the head. I automatically smiled and shook their hands. They left satisfied there were no German soldiers hiding in the house and no weapons. We really did not have any.

When the front door closed with a bang my mother and I looked at each other in silence. We had played a dangerous game. We understood each other. We were a team. But there were more Russian search parties. What would the next lot do? There was no more brandy. In years to come I saw in pictures and later on the TV how various populations greeted incoming victorious armies; they all cheered, threw flowers and all that. So did we, instinctively. It works. But I give brandy the thumbs up over flowers.

Next, still without rest or sleep and with the smell of burning hanging in the air and the continuing rumble of tanks, I was sent to help my grandmother in the barn to feed the rabbits. There were no more POWs to do this. You may find this odd, but we worried about our POWs. How would they fare? Not well, it turned out. The rabbits were accommodated in rows of houses four and five tiers high.

My grandfather believed in giving the animals maximum height cages so that they could stand up on their hind legs. That meant the top rabbits had to be attended to by using a ladder. That's why I was needed and the hay had to be thrown down from a high-level floor to the ground using a giant fixed wooden ladder. Oh, was that a hard job. I managed, of course, as there was no one else to help.

Suddenly we heard exhausted panting and fast running steps and one of our Poles burst through the barn gate. He gasped that he was being followed by Russian soldiers. His language must have given him away, because when our POWs left we had given them what clothes we had from my father and uncles, so no one could have identified them by their uniform with POW printed on the back. Sure enough, through one of the narrow windows on the top level of the barn, I could see emerging from the forest two figures running towards the house, still about 400 metres away. My grandmother was back to her quick thinking, practical self. At the back of the barn in a corner stood a giant wooden box, a good metre high, about one and half metres wide and two metres long. It was kept full of bran for the rabbits and several sacks of bran stood in front of it.

'Quick, child, give me a hand.' She ushered our Pole into the box, I helped – putting empty sacking on him, then emptying more sacks with bran on top. I closed the lid and now, quick, child, feed the rabbits with hay, pretend nothing out of the ordinary has happened. I started doing just that not a second too early. The two Russian soldiers rushed in. They looked furious, obviously having lost their quarry. They shouted questions which we did not understand. They ran crisscross through the barn. My grandmother remained very calm, looked attentive, indicated that she meant to be helpful and I was trembling with fear and switched on automatic. I stuffed handful after handful of hay into the same rabbit hatch, the poor things could no longer move. The two soldiers were a terrible sight. Their uniforms so incredibly dirty, like a person who has lived in muck for ages without ever getting a wash. The material of their clothes and their faces shone like glistening mud, but they were shaved.

The whole situation was so alien and shattering that I started to cry again, even if quietly. '*Weine nicht, mein Kindchen,*' said my grandmother. Don't cry, my little child. One of the soldiers turned to me and stroked my hair and he spoke some soothing words. Under all that dirt there was a human being. And yet, he and his comrade would most probably have killed our Pole. Human nature is so hard to understand. To be honest, I understood nothing. We had always kept our yard free from snow, so the footsteps of our Pole could not be followed and the two Russians left our property. God help us if they had found him. We would all have been dead.

More soldiers searched our house; some were violent, we were pushed about with their weapons, my great-grandfather was beaten up. My mother was as co-operative as possible, anticipating their every move, she flung open all doors and cupboards and wardrobes to show that no one was hiding and that there were no weapons anywhere.

We were all in a state of high alarm and virtually on the point of collapse through hunger and sleeplessness. My little brothers, sister and cousins were too scared to cry and too hungry, thirsty and weak to do anything, they just lay there on sofas and beds not moving. That same evening my grandmother suffered a heart attack. I did not know then what it was. I was full of sadness for her, but felt mainly overwhelming sorrow for my mother. She now turned out to be an Amazonian, she kept going like a robot and her requests became commands to be obeyed promptly by everyone. Everyone in the house accepted her as our leader unquestioningly. There were brief periods of rest that night, the sky red with flames, the whole town by now burning, the rumble of tanks continuing unabated. Whenever there was a knock on our substantial front door, it was my mother who opened it, showing no fear. Fear can trigger violence but my mother had iron control over herself.

My grandmother had been bedded down in great-grandfather's bed, it was the quietest part of the house. Great-grandfather was staying with her and she was unconscious. My mother had started picking up Russian words that mattered from day one. She noticed that some soldiers when coming near grandmother's bed had uttered something like '*mamooshka*', presumably being the diminutive of 'mother'. Many of the soldiers became somewhat softer in their dealings with us, so my mother thought granny might perhaps save us and took all new search parties first to granny's bed, where her mamooshka was apparently dying. It worked. Virtually all battle-hardened soldiers quietened down and the occasional one even stroked her hair. What grieved me so was my great-grandfather crying about his little Annchen, little Annie. She was his youngest child. He was 85 years old. I could do nothing but stroke his hand.

Search parties kept coming. Some were very rough and violent, my poor great-grandfather was singled out and beaten up. If you were a German man you were beaten up, that was standard treatment. He was brave and did not want to hide and said at least it deflected violence away from us, but my mother was not having any more of it and persuaded him to hide in our secret cellar. Without light and in the cold down there it was an ordeal, but he had more chance of survival there than in the house with us. Our bomb shelter would have been better, as it was equipped with everything one would need to survive for a few days with tolerable discomfort. But the garden and entrance to it were covered with snow and footsteps leading to the shelter would have given the hiding place away.

My uncle and aunt who had fled from Poland a few years ago fled to our house on 3 February following a horrific killing spree in their house. Most people in their house had been Polish refugees, that was their downfall. It was noticeable that the Russian soldiers hunted down Polish people. It was irrational, unbelievable, what on earth had the Russian leaders indoctrinated their soldiers with? The Poles had not been traitors, nor were they collaborators with the Germans, they had merely run for their lives, run away from Zhukow's army. I began to understand the reaction of our Polish POWs on hearing that the Russians were coming closer to our area.

One day, early in February, I went outside to play in the yard. I had a little boy with me who was about six years old, he was the son of refugees staying with us. We were bombarding a tree with snowballs to see who could achieve the most hits. It was fun. The snow was so cold that it had to be kneaded to make it pliable or the snowballs would not clump together. A Russian soldier appeared in the driveway leading to our yard and took pot shots at us. Little Richard fell down in the snow, dead.

At that moment I felt again somewhat irrational, everything was so unreal; I became mad. I lived in a bubble that no one could pierce. I could dance and laugh and scream in front of gunfire. It would not hit me. I could and would be so provocative in months to come, so daring, take so many risks, and yet at the end of it all I did indeed walk away from that mortal danger against all odds and I lived to tell the story.

I calmly walked back into the house and said, 'They have shot little Richard.' I felt so bad because I had persuaded him to come outside and play with me. I tried to work out what makes a human being shoot at children. A German child was then worth nothing and shooting German children was certainly more fun than a pheasant shoot, easier anyway. And how many have shot children of other nationalities? Why does the human race produce these psychos? Well, it is a problem I cannot comprehend and therefore cannot solve. Has anyone ever come up with an answer? The real difficulty lies in not being able to tell at a glance who is good and who is bad and who is a real psychopath, at least I can't, not until it is perhaps too late.

That day was a bad day anyway. German planes had been overhead and the Russians had installed an anti-aircraft device in an abandoned railway wagon, to me it looked like a cannon with an extra-long barrel. The railway line ran, as I said before, through our fields where I had once waved my Daddy goodbye. The German planes were obviously homing in on the apparently never-ending succession of tanks going through our town with no manoeuvrability and limited means of defence if attacked from the air. The German planes then left the area all at once. The Russian anti-aircraft position had been detected and what followed was one of my most frightening experiences of the war simply in terms of the awful noise, not to mention the resulting destruction. I knew from pictures virtually all German planes plus the better known enemy ones. Stukas were approaching. We watched in fear. Stukas had a terrible reputation. One plane peeled off from the formation and with a most terrible screaming sound it seemed to plunge to the ground. The railway wagons with their stored ammunition splintered with a deafening, fiery explosion. The shock wave nearly lifted us off our feet and the tiles of a large part of our house were dislodged.

Breathing became difficult, we had been too close to the impact and our lungs had taken quite a pounding. There was no more firing from the railway line. Everything had disappeared. I had wet myself. I felt as if I had put my finger into an electric socket, making all of my hair stand on end. The worst effect was the disorientation induced by the Stuka's scream. I just could not get my thoughts together, I could not react and was at an utter loss as to what to do next. I was grabbed by my mother and dragged to safety back into the house where little Richard's body still lay on the kitchen table. He was later buried under the apple tree where I had sat as a toddler enjoying spring for the first time in my life.

My uncle tried that afternoon to re-lay the tiles on our roof, but as he was shot at he dived down between the rafters and gave up for the time being. It had been a bad day so far, with more to come. More Russian search parties arrived; or more accurately, pilfering parties. If you could unearth some food you were well away and to hell with everyone else. If you could snatch valuables you might be able to swap them for food, so they were also welcome. And if you were German and still wore your wedding ring or a watch or anything else of value then you were stupid and could only blame yourself for having them snatched. Such items should have been well wrapped and dug in somewhere long before, for someone to find them in a few hundred years' time. The Russian soldiers understood a few days after their arrival there was no more to be had because 'comrades have already been here before you.'

On that particular day two really vicious types turned up. They rampaged through everything and continued their search in the sheds and barn. We had a large wash and utility house with two very large cauldrons, enamel-lined and built into wood-fired hearths. They held about 50 litres each. Only one was for washing. We made jam on a large scale in the other, the contents were stirred with an enormous wooden spoon, looking like a paddle. Jam making took hours, have the fire too low and the jam would not sufficiently boil and not set, have it too hot and it would burn. I remember that wonderful aroma of black plum jam and strawberry jam. Strawberries were grown by the acre.

Well, back to that dreadful day. These two soldiers were trouble. They rummaged through the cauldrons as well. In one of them under dirty washing my mother had hidden the big salami which we had brought back from Küstrin. As they walked past us, one of them with the salami in his hand, my mother rushed forward and snatched it from him and retreated up the steps to our front door where I stood. The soldiers were enraged and a fierce tug of war broke out. My mother did not let go of the sausage although one of the soldiers, apparently an officer, thumped her repeatedly. My mother fought like a lioness. Suddenly, the officer drew a very long, thin-bladed sword — possibly it was not even called a sword, it was curved towards the tip and looked more like the weapons wielded by cavalry I had seen on old paintings, a sabre perhaps? — anyway, with an outburst of horrible swear words in Russian, which we had learned within a day, he raised it high ready to strike. My mother instinctively raised her salami in defence. I hung on to her skirt with both hands trying to tug her away. I will never forget that sight. A very big man and a slight woman each grabbing the other's clothes for purchase and with a weapon raised high in their right hand. A sword against a salami. The salami won. The other soldier pulled his officer away from us, constantly talking to him and they walked away. The hate-filled face of the officer was unforgettable.

My mother would have been the first to recognise that her action was not bravery but an unthinking response, it was a bluff. It might work, it might not. Most of the time, as I observed throughout life, the bluff works. The outcome is worth the gamble; the salami was cut up and eaten there and then. No one could have it any more.

Pity, insofar as salami is durable and would have kept for much longer for a real emergency.

After that incident more people in our house, relatives and refugees alike, crammed into our secret cellar. It was unlikely that the cellar would be found, it ran along one of the outer walls with ventilation shafts well covered by shrubbery outside. In an emergency you could claw your way out of it under cover of darkness. But we could not, of course, put my bedridden grandmother underground. She was still not fully conscious, she needed warmth and care and I was curled up fully dressed as always in a large armchair next to her bed, always on full alert and ready to leap into action at the slightest sound. We only spoke in hushed voices, my mother bravely opening the front door at the slightest knock. Her self-control was remarkable, if you looked frightened, the soldiers would have it in for you. Why should you be frightened of the Russian army? That was an insult. If you looked defiant, you were dead. She kept up a kind of neutral expression with a hint of welcome, with very calm, unhurried movements.

There were also, as everywhere in the world, intelligent and compassionate officers and privates among the Russian soldiers, some speaking very good German. Some stayed for long talks and a hot drink. Everyone was always frozen, the outside temperatures were bitter that winter. These soldiers abhorred war and violence as we did, like every decent human being. The soldiers explained that their comrades had come from Mongolia. We had been wondering about these large numbers of Asian-looking men, that they were not used to houses, furniture and the like, neither were they made to live in barracks, when available. They lived in tents or dug outs and they were masters at building them. These Asiatic soldiers were fretful; no wonder, they moved in a world they were not accustomed to. They were very dangerous and violent (which is what every successful army really needs!). There was a very uneasy, quite complex relationship between them and the comparatively large number of Poles in our area.

Apparently, it worked like this. First to arrive were the punishment battalions, then Asians and Poles. They were the cannon fodder, commanded by Russian officers. So some of the first to arrive were large numbers from the far eastern part of the Russian empire. Curiously, troops from the very east of Siberia looked very European, I would imagine people from Finland and Sweden to look like this with a mix from the northern Ukraine, or the Don area. Presumably they were descendants from the early settlers of Siberia who ventured as far as the Bering Strait. They seemed to have taken their Slavonic language with them. There were also many from Belarus. That was roughly the make-up of the Russian army in our area, that's the best I can do. As a child I was fascinated by their different looks and height and size, but had, of course, no idea of the huge population variety of the vast country they represented.

My mother was very open minded and often engaged in lively conversation with some of the men, mainly German speaking officers, while making rounds of hot drinks. The drinks consisted of hot water thickened with a spoonful of oatmeal sweetened with homemade syrup from sugar beet. Many times we shook hands with them when they left, they wished us well, we wished them well, we all hoped the war would soon be over and life would get better for everyone. Well, it might for some. Not, of course, if you are the loser. You will meet hatred at every turn, you will be accused of and punished for things you have never done. The majority of the winners would dance with joy on the graves of the vanquished, in this case any German, man, woman or child. Such an attitude was shown to me throughout my life, to my despair and that of the honourable, good people of all nationalities. And often those that judged and punished the so-called guilty were more ruthless and cruel than the ones they punished.

In those desperate early days of February 1945 some women (German men no longer seemed to exist) acted as a kind of walking newspaper. They were very brave, they had usually already lost most or all of their family and with only their own lives at stake, acted as messengers. If you wanted to find out what might have happened to your daughter, your mother, father, uncle, son, friend or whoever, last seen in such and such a village, they would go out and gather information.

They learned large numbers of names, dates, addresses and dodging soldiers and bullets kept communication going between families. From one of them we heard that my blonde Ingeborg and her family, including everyone in their house, had been shot on 2 February. Irene and her family and everyone in their house had also been shot. I remember Irene's father had been declared unfit for service because he was very short-sighted. He was a biologist or scientist with a special interest in insects and butterflies. Their house was full of framed, preserved butterflies; he also painted them. So, my two friends and their families were now dead. I was still there and so was Lizzy. But we did not hear anything about Lizzy. I must admit that I became very frightened by all this devastating news; one inevitably thinks, when will be my last day? We also heard that the two dentists in our town and their families had been shot. That will teach you to be German and in the Party. Our two doctors, a father and son team, had been murdered, reportedly stabbed. They too had been in the Party. Had they not been members of course, they could not have practised.

Now what could you do when you needed expert advice on how to keep alive when you had suffered multiple injuries? The most common injuries were sustained from serious beatings, the outcome was mostly fatal, with or without help. But occasionally with the correct know-how, survival was possible. Hatred is so destructive. My grandfather was right. According to the Ancient Greeks even gods fight stupidity in vain. More horror stories circulated. More friends of ours had been shot and their houses burnt. The family who owned the wood yard and the horses we worked with had been murdered. Apparently during a violent rampage through their home, one woman had drawn a revolver and aimed it at a Russian soldier; she must have lost her nerve. With five children to protect she had clearly lost the plot. The last thing you do in such a situation is to invite execution. All grown-ups in that house were shot. The children were untouched; only to be burnt alive in the house. We found this unbelievable. What happened next?

During another cruel rampage that same day in the home of our nearest grocer, overspilling with refugees as well, a mother of five children drew a revolver and took a pot shot from a top window at soldiers in the street. All grown-ups in the house were killed, the house then set on fire, the children screaming from the second-floor windows. One woman who had escaped came racing to our home yelling for help for the children. My mother, two of my aunties and my uncle rushed there as fast as they could. They were beaten and held back by the soldiers, unable to do anything to save the children. Never mind going to hell if you have been bad. The suffering and pain is your own. To have to endure the suffering of little children without being able to come to their assistance and having to abandon them is a torture in quite a different category. My aunties and uncle returned in a state of shock, crying hysterically. My mother was shivering and vomited a lot. My great-grandfather cuddled her like a child.

When it was dark, people in our house came up from the cellar to share some sort of hot soup. Before they could get back down there was again that dreaded knock on the front door. My mother opened it. In came an officer and two privates. After that catastrophe at the grocer's they were looking for weapons. They ushered everyone, including us children, into the hall. There were so many people crowded in the hall that some women stayed on the stairs. There were about two dozen of us assembled. The soldiers shouted at us in Russian, but nobody understood. One woman on the stairs began to cry with fright. The officer stepped closer to her, pulled out a Cossack whip and started flailing her. Such a whip is made of plaited leather and like long plaited hair it tapers towards the end. These whips cut through clothing and flesh. The woman screamed in terror and pain. The two soldiers now started thumping and punching other women and they now began crying loudly. The children whimpered. I remember standing motionless, my eyes on my mother.

She stepped forward, quietly, towards the officer. She put her left hand on the officer's upper arm, with her right hand she stroked his right hand that held the whip. She started speaking, her voice calm and even. She told him not to be afraid, no one would do any harm to him or his men and that it was wrong for a big, strong man like him to whip a helpless woman. She continued to speak to him along these lines for a little while. He stood there as if frozen, listening. He did not understand German, my mother did not understand Russian. The officer appeared to relax, he looked my mother full in the face in silence. Then he spoke a few words to the two soldiers and they left.

After only a little while – we were still in the hall – there was that feared knock on the door again. We all thought, oh no, they have come back for revenge. My mother opened the door. The officer stepped in, looked around, searching for my mother. When he recognised her, he put his whip without saying a word into her hands, bowed, turned and left. When you think what horrors and sights this man had lived through before reaching our door, it is a measure of his humanity that he was able to pull himself back from the brink. All the world had gone mad; but here was a man who was not prepared to be consumed by this insanity.

There was a sigh of relief all round. My reaction was different. I had witnessed a moment of greatness. My admiration for my mother would be ever present throughout my life. Here was a person who could save us, if it was at all possible during those horrendous times. One needed luck, a lot of luck, backed up by someone who could assess human strength and frailty instantly and make the correct judgement without fail every time.

We talked about dying, perhaps today we might die. It seemed inevitable and although it was not our fault, we would have to accept it. I remember hoping that it would not hurt too much. And I felt so sorry for my Daddy, who after the war might never find out what happened to us. If my mother could not stop us getting killed, no one could. I found this strangely soothing.

As for the whip, it was well hidden in a dry place in the house to show Daddy. We could not afford another search party to find such a whip in our possession. If the house is still there, the whip will be there. No one will have found it. But I could go back to our house and go straight to the place where it is.

The daily torment went on, the town continued to burn, the sound of tanks rumbled on day and night, we forgot my youngest brother's birthday, we forgot my eldest brother's birthday, the soft toys which I had helped to make for these occasions were never given.

People were chased from their houses because the Russians were suffering a great number of casualties as the fighting along the Oder river intensified. Most of our town centre had by now been burnt to cinders and the outlying properties were needed as emergency hospitals. Rumour had it that the entire town, or what was left of it, would be cleared as shelter for Russian troops. We now saw more European faces among the soldiers, confirming our first impression of the universal battle strategy: punishment battalions first, Asians and Poles as cannon fodder second, then European Russians. It makes sense, doesn't it?

Many people fled from their houses into the forest or anywhere to escape the daily visitations by soldiers. Most in our house left; they panicked understandably, but in my mother's view acted unwisely. What will you do without shelter, fire, food or drink in temperatures between -12°C to -20°C? And it gets colder during the night. I was only a child and even with my limited judgement I did not give anyone a chance of survival. With my grandmother so ill and at times so confused that she did not recognise us, it was best to stay undercover in our own place, where we knew every nook and cranny. But that was taken from us as well.

It was 13 February when a group of Russian soldiers went from house to house to tell us to go, to go east; they wanted us gone by the time they came back, which was in minutes. Their German was poor but clear. It consisted of the words 'dawai, dawai', if you can call that German, but if you were poked with weapons in the back, then dawai could only mean 'get out, fast'. We were all brilliant linguists. On that day our entire town was cleared early in the morning. Thousands of civilians were turned out into the bitter winter. It is bad enough for reasonably well clad men with army provisions to fight in ice and snow, it is far worse for women with children and babies, for the sick and the old to be tossed out into the freezing conditions, with inadequate clothing, without food or blankets and already suffering from hunger, ill treatment and beatings. At the same time they are fair game and at the mercy of every psychopath, every pervert, every paedophile, everyone with criminal leanings, murderers, such men encouraged in their actions by those who feel just in declaring that any crime against a German is quite acceptable and, in fact, a good deed. The Germans deserve it. They are wicked and evil.

I am a pretty average person, so other people, whatever nationality, must be as wicked and evil as I am. One has to try to pick oneself up and show the world that it can be different. It is so hard, so hard. I feel such sorrow for the many who could go no farther, who had come to the end of what they could endure and then wilted under the pressure of cruelty, loss of loved ones and total indifference to their sufferings, and who then committed suicide to find some peace. Life had crushed them and had taken every defence away from them. I was aware of that and it has caused me great sadness as a child and later in life.

RAUS! UHODI!

Back to the moment when the soldiers forced us to abandon our home. My aunties helped to get my brothers dressed for the out-doors. I dressed myself in the warmest clothes that were ready to hand, double cardigans, gloves, shawls. I stuffed underwear and socks into my pockets. To my great shame and regret I neglected to take care of my little sister. On hearing that we had to be outside where it might be dirty, she changed her good clothes for old ones, even left her warm new, fur-lined winter coat behind, which had only just been made up for her in December 1944. She had put on her old one which was too short in the sleeves and did not cover her knees and was too tight to wear a cardigan under it. With that her fate was sealed. I was stunned when I realised it, but it was too late: the Russians were coming back.

My mother loaded my grandmother into a hand cart with the help of great-grandfather, with some blankets and emergency food and a pot to boil water in, some aluminium bowls and some knives.

You don't need forks, you don't need spoons, you can drink from a bowl, but you need fire-making equipment, a pot and a knife. We could not take much in the cart, our most valuable luggage was grandmama. Wheels are next to useless in snow, but our children's sleighs were too small to be loaded with goods and a large one had to be drawn by a horse. So my mother ended up pulling the wheels through, rather than over, the snow. We were already on the front steps ready to go with the soldiers in sight on their way back when my mother pulled me back into the house. She opened the door to one of the living rooms, the furniture still there, the glass cabinets with most of her favourite china collection still intact. She loved china, Japanese porcelain in particular. My father's medieval glass collection and tankards were all still in one piece. She said, 'Quick, have a look. You will never see anything like this again.' She was right. I remember quite clearly all those precious and rich memories of our house, our home and our lives. Running back to the front door we were stopped by great-grandfather, who pulled my mother into his rooms. He was also a fine china collector. He unlocked a glass cabinet and took from a jug a piece of paper. 'Take this,' he said to my mother, 'it is the address of our New York relatives. I have kept in touch, write to them as soon as you can, they will help you.' My mother took the address and then he said 'Goodbye, all of you. I am not coming with you. I am a liability. You already have my Annchen.' No time to waste. The soldiers were already in the yard. We hurried away. Our other relatives were not yet ready, not all were young and fit enough to dress themselves for outdoors.

My mother more dragged than pulled the cart forward, my brothers and sister walking while hanging on to the cart. The snow was high and I pushed from the back. We made for the forest through the orchard at the end of our long field that would lead us to the road to Soldin. Halfway across our field I stopped and turned round to have a last look at our house. There, on the top of our doorstep, stood my beloved great-grandfather with one hand over his face, clearly crying. With the other hand he was waving us goodbye with his large white hanky. There was nothing I could do. He had survived the 1870/71 war as a drummer boy, he was called up just as he left school. He was 11 when he left school. He survived the 1914–18 war, he would not see the end of this one. When I saw him last, he had only hours to live; his end has haunted us ever since. Of my other close relatives who were in the house on that day, I saw only two again briefly in the coming three weeks, shortly before their deaths. None of the others were ever heard of or seen again.

My mother's objective was clear. With small children to care for and a very sick mother, she was waiting for no one. To get us off the road to somewhere sheltered and safe before dark was her aim. On our way to the Soldiner Chaussee we passed the house of very dear close relatives of ours. They also had young children. They were not yet ready to leave, the orders to get out had only just reached them. My mother did not wait. I saw my dearest cousin, younger than me, for the last time on that day. That family survived like us against all odds and about sixty years later my little cousin and I managed to get in touch again after the fall of the Berlin Wall. And when we write to each other it is as if we have never been parted, it feels like having a conversation over a cup of coffee. We would not recognise each other if we were to meet in the street. We are now too old and unfit and too far apart ever to visit each other, but our thinking and our views about the world are so alike; in spite of having spent our lives in totally different ideological regimes, we know we are family.

We said a hasty goodbye, my grandmother only half conscious in the cart, and we set off for the town of Soldin. My mother reasoned that with thousands of people on the road in the open, so many would fall by the wayside that most would end up in the villages closest to our town. This would mean desperate overcrowding and, as a consequence, no food. So, her aim was to get as far away as possible as quickly as possible from our town, to where people would be more thinly spread and there would be more chance of finding shelter and food. Her reasoning was spot on and her determination unshakeable. I had a good grasp of her absolutely ruthless willpower. I heard her talk to herself aloud. Again and again: 'How will I explain to you that I did not get the children out of this?' She was, of course, talking to my Daddy, wherever in the world he was. And the distance she intended to walk with us today? About 35km. Without food, with a heavy cart, a helpless mother and four children, of whom only I could be of some use. We were not even out of town, only about 3km away from our home, when I did come in useful. Very young, ill-nourished children cannot walk far and my little brothers could not stumble on any longer, so one was put on top of granny and the other was lifted on to my back. I carried him for at least 30km that day. My little sister had no one to carry her, nor could she be put into the cart. That dear little girl trudged bravely on her thin little legs all day through ice and snow. She never even cried.

As we were approaching the Soldiner Chaussee the extent of the horror that had befallen the survivors of the 1944 population of about 25,000 was exposed. Amid the snow and ice, icicles hanging from the high branches of the forest on either side, a slow-moving line of thousands of people, mainly women and children, was trudging forward with no beginning nor end in sight. Bent under the weight of children on their backs like me, meagre items of food, sick children, dying children and other relatives too dear to be abandoned were pushed, pulled, dragged and carried along on the left-hand side of the road crawling east. On the right-hand side were tanks going west, one after the other, endlessly.

Many could not cope, they collapsed crying or just sat by the wayside staring with empty eyes at the moving mass of humanity passing them by. They were waiting for death, which came soon enough. We passed hundreds of bodies lying on the road. Some people had been out on that stretch of road hours or days before and were now dead, frozen solid, sometimes in heaps of four, five and more. Some had been shot, some beaten to death, others with their heads crushed to pulp, otherwise in one piece. Once their bodies had been covered by snow, but were now exposed. If you wanted to go forwards you had to step on them, push your cart over them. It is hard enough to walk along a slippery road due to ice and compacted snow, worse to have to step up onto a body, then down again, then up again onto the next one, getting colder and colder, hungrier and hungrier, feeling weaker and weaker, without an end or rest in sight. You begin to wonder how long you can endure this mental and physical torture and consider how nice it would be just to sit down and have a little sleep for a while, regardless of the consequences.

Occasionally some soldiers would jump off a tank and take a blanket or coat off someone. Here and there were some Poles, trying to hide themselves among us Germans, trying to go home. Home was east. Being men, they had to disguise themselves and some dressed as women. For some reason the Russians singled them out and brutally murdered them. A terrible fear gripped us all when such unspeakable bestialities took place, but we were too paralysed to cry or utter a sound. There was an uncanny silence enveloping all in the vicinity as another human being was turned into ice to be stepped over by those who followed. And it seemed so likely that you yourself would be next.

While I am trying not to dwell on such images because I may pass my nightmares onto an unsuspecting reader, I think I will mention another incident, which is still as clear as crystal in my mind. Tanks drive on in a straight line. When they meet an obstacle they don't drive around it. They are not designed for small detours, although capable of it. So, if anyone stumbles, slips or collapses into the path of a tank, that unfortunate will be turned into a red stain on the road and no one need step over it any more. When I witnessed such an unimaginable scene for the first time, I literally forgot to breathe. I froze, unable to move, shocked. I remember my mother rushing over to me and thumping me hard on my shoulder and chest as I had my brother on my back. I heard her shout as if from far away, 'Walk on, child, walk on, we cannot help them any more, walk on.' And I walked on from one terrible scene to another. I saw without seeing, numbed and chilled and not daring to cry. Neither did my little sister and there was no sound made by my little brothers. One had forgotten to take his teddy. I remember he asked for it once. My mother told him teddy was at home and fast asleep in his bed. My brother never asked again. Teddy was safe. I also never forgot my little sister's ever so dark blue, big, hungry eyes.

After about 20km or so there were fewer people on the road, only the hardy like my mother were still trudging on. Most had fallen by the wayside. Few would survive the night. It was getting quite dark now and words fail me to describe the degree of exhaustion and fear that was gripping me. Unless something happened to give us a glimmer of hope we were done for. We were lucky, the glimmer materialised. In the darkness the sky began to glow, redder and brighter with every kilometre that we stumbled on. The town of Soldin was resolving itself into a glowing sunrise. We followed the glow like the three kings followed the star of Bethlehem. Perhaps around midnight, we approached the outskirts of the town. And here I saw another weapon which frightened the wits out of me. Looming dark and towering well above the height of a nearby house stood a massive Flak gun. The mere size of it conveyed its destructive power and I suffered another panic attack and, being so tired, I even cried. The by now familiar 'walk on, child, walk on' sounded in my ears and on I went.

Finding shelter proved to be difficult. We stumbled through row after row of completely destroyed houses, many still burning, it looked more like a bomb attack than accident or arson. The area we had entered was completely deserted and we did not know which way to turn. There seemed to be no way out either, with roads blocked by collapsed buildings and we were quite disorientated. I was thinking of the Minotaur's maze. A small dark figure emerged from a half-destroyed building. A feeble voice pleaded: please, please, help me. I am alone, please, stay with me. A trembling old woman approached us. She, like my great-grandfather, had been left behind when her family had fled. We were only too glad to go with her. Part of her house was still standing. The top half had departed and the front caved in. But round the side was a good-sized hole in the brick wall and we clambered in. The room still had a ceiling and through another hole in an opposite wall there was another room, also with a ceiling. The second room was more sheltered. I helped my mother to get granny inside; the three young children were laid down on a bed with loads of bedding and blankets provided by the dear old woman.

My mother constructed a simple hearth from loose bricks, she 'cooked' delicious hot water, we could thaw out and also had a meagre ration of bread.

Much later I learned that this was the night that Dresden was firebombed out of existence. And I don't believe the low figures given after the war for the numbers of people killed during the raid. Dresden, like my own town, would have accommodated several times more refugees than the original number of people living there. Moreover, I don't think that the Germans expected the town to be bombed and enormous numbers of evacuees, among them orphans and lost children from all over Germany, had been sent there by the tens of thousands. Dresden was considered safe, being a jewel of European civilization and had minimal defences. I will say more about Dresden later on. That night I sank into oblivion.

Our plight re-emerged with unforgiving clarity the following morning. 'I am not going to stay,' I heard my mother say. 'There will be no food anywhere in this area. I must move on with the children.' 'And I am not going with you,' said my grandmother. 'It will be beyond your strength to take me as well, and you must save the children. I will be a handicap to you. Load the children into the cart and leave, this is my last word.' My mother agreed that this was the only sensible option open to her.

We dressed for the road, had a piece of bread and hot water. The old woman assured us that she would look after our grandmother, she was very anxious to keep her as company, but their fate could not be taken into consideration by my mother. My mother and her mother had only one thing to consider: the children's survival. We children said our innocent goodbyes and scrambled through the hole in the wall. I was last. As I clambered over the bricks I suddenly remembered that it was the birthday of my grandmother. I hastily stumbled back and walked up to her. She was sitting on the floor, still too weak to stand. I remembered my manners. I curtsied and wished her a happy birthday. There was a smile on her face, which I could not interpret and she said, '*Mein liebes Kind, leb wohl.*' My dear child, farewell. I quickly left and joined my mother. It was my job to help push the cart.

It was only then that I realised the extraordinary nature of that moment of goodbye. The contrast between happy birthdays in the past, with my granny so ill now and sitting on the floor in a bombed-out house, us outside on an icy road, homeless, surrounded by enemy troops in the middle of winter, was so stark that I began to shed bitter tears.

We found our way out of town quickly. On the outskirts of the town we saw a few houses still intact which my mother thought were worth investigating, some might call it looting. The investigation was completed hastily, the sound of planes was in the air and the one thing you never do is to go into a building that is still standing and looking undamaged, because that building will be the target and civilians in those days were the target. We were in luck. My mother had found a side of smoked pork that someone had to leave behind, probably running for their lives. Well, their misfortune was our food.

Unbelievably, when walking on, we saw ahead of us on the road my uncle who had been arrested and his wife, who once had held the secret dinner parties in her kitchen. What a joy and relief for us. My mother had help pulling the cart and having company we felt better equipped to deal with the dangers ahead.

I think we were on the road leading to Renitz a few kilometres away from Soldin. I think Renitz, or Rhenitz, was a small village. I remember a crushed road sign lying on the ground. It was perhaps a distance of only 6km or so. These 6km took us all day. I don't know how best to put the events of this day into words. I will try to give account in the simplest way.

We shared the road with the Russian army going west, as before. They drove past us in many different types of vehicles, anything from tanks right down to the humble horse and cart. But this particular lot looked more Asian; that in itself was not disquieting, but unfortunately on that road we ran into a particularly cruel group. Only a short distance out of Soldin we came across their first victims. A group of six or seven people, partly stripped naked, beaten to a pulp. I swallowed hard. Two to three hundred metres on, another group, women and children treated the same way, on the opposite side of the road another group. And so on. To the right, to the left, the tragic sight of massacred humanity. There was no point in walking back to town. The Russians were going that way. You cannot stay put in the middle of the road either. There was nothing for it but put one foot in front of the other. We continued with hearts in our mouths. We passed many more scenes of atrocious murder, we kept our eyes down, the Russians drove past us and over the bodies. Frankly, there was nowhere else to go but over them. If you were a bad person you did not care and if you were a good person, then there was nothing you could do about it.

We came to another heap of bodies and I stopped. Some had been so badly beaten that I could not make out whether the bloody mess in front of me had once been male or female. I felt my mother's hand on my shoulder and heard her say, 'Come on, child, we are too late, we cannot help them anymore. Walk on.' And I walked on. After a few minutes the road was only occupied by us and other refugees. No Russians. Then there was the sound of returning planes in the air. We had a bad feeling about this; these were not bombers, they were fighter aircraft, obviously with some unspent ammunition on board. And sure enough, they came straight for us: refugees, women and children.

Well, I had seen them in action before, so don't do what they expect you to do. Don't run for cover in to the ditches on either side of the road, that's what they are aiming for. While my mother, auntie and uncle threw themselves over the cart with the three children, I ran out into the field covered by frozen snow. A plane cannot turn at sharp angles, you can see them coming, you can see the stream of bullets on the ground, you can outrun them if you have the space to do it and a single person is not a worthwhile target to pursue. But first you must have seen them operate, you must be fit and able to put your previous observations to good use. Above all, you must be a very lucky person to survive it. I did. We did. Most of the others did not.

There were so many injured, there was much crying, many collapsed with grief and despair. 'Come on, hurry up,' my mother shouted.

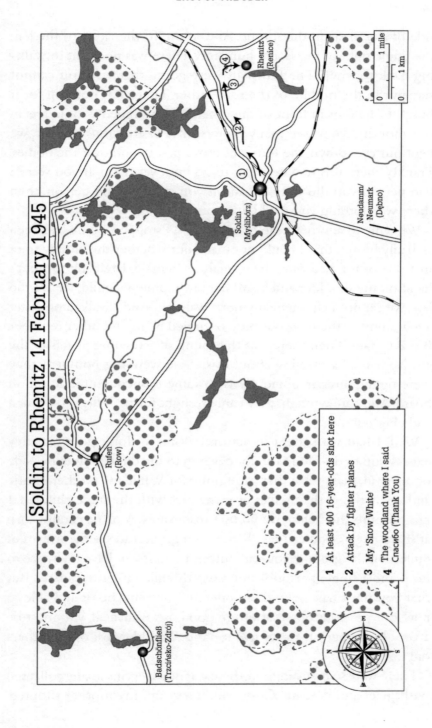

Soldin to Rhenitz 14 February 1945

Rhenitz
(Renice)

4

3

2

Soldin
(Myślibórz)

1

Neudamm/
Neumark
(Dębno)

Rufen
(Rów)

Badschönfließ
(Trzcińsko-Zdrój)

1 At least 400 16-year-olds shot here
2 Attack by fighter planes
3 My 'Snow White'
4 The woodland where I said
Спасибо (Thank You)

1 mile
1 km
0
0

'We must get off this road.' We saw a small woodland to the right ahead of us and made for it as fast as we could. My thoughts were in turmoil. Why, oh why, would the planes attack us? We were in no position to do anyone any harm. Our plight was so obvious, even from above. We must have been a pitiful sight. The war was surely over and won by now, so why continue with this senseless murder of civilians?

After the war I found that our noble victors were just ordinary human beings, like us. Most were good, but some people are truly malicious and once unrestrained by law and order they can cause unimaginable carnage.

We had only progressed a few hundred metres when we were halted by an armoured vehicle; one soldier jumped off. Our hearts stopped and I heard my mother murmur: 'Oh please, let them have the mercy to kill the children before me.' We were in luck again. The soldier walked up to my uncle, indicated that he wanted his warm jacket, which was given. The soldier put it on himself and hopped back on to his vehicle. What a relief. But never underestimate the effect of severe cold on a person without warm clothing.

We had to stop again before we reached the woodland, the road was blocked by bodies. The usual. Violated women, naked bodies, brute force used to kill men, or rather boys, women and children snuffed out as if they were vermin. And even vermin should be killed without having to endure terror and pain. One person had tried to run away onto the snow-covered fields, a young boy, about 14 or 15 years old. They had caught up with him, he had been mercilessly beaten and then had his throat cut. The blood had not yet frozen, but the boy was dead. I have never felt so helpless. No matter how much I wanted to comfort and help him. It was no use. He was dead. I started to cry and cried as I had never done before. I cried for the boy. I cried for the cruelty of man to man. I cried for myself. This moment was also the farewell to my childhood. The era of fairy tales, of love and security, had gone. There was my Snow White, with hair as black as ebony, with skin as white as snow, with lips as red as blood. I was inconsolable and did not know how to stop crying.

You can go on crying without tears. You can call it a nervous break-down. But you have to go on walking if you want to live. After that I never cried again until much later.

We reached the woodland and now, partially hidden from sight, breathed a little easier. We were not the only visitors there. There was a small group of Russian soldiers, they had lit a fire and were cooking a meal for themselves. They were very friendly and kind, we children were arranged round the fire and the grown-ups had a go at conversation, using their hands more than words, helped by the knowledge of Polish of my uncle and aunt. The common consensus was, war was 'nix gut'. The dinner was ready. Russian army rations were desperately poor and the dinner consisted of the ubiquitous cabbage. But not like the cabbage that you know, this cabbage was garbage. Frozen, thawed and going off. It has its very own distinctive smell, it stinks. But hot stinking cabbage boiled in water is delicious when there is nothing else. The kind soldiers shared their dinner with us.

It was obvious that I was still very distressed. One kind hearted soldier patted me on the back and got me a soft cuddly toy. A red squirrel bounced through the branches, he shot it for me. Alas he missed, only its tail fell off and the soldier retrieved it and with a big smile gave it to me. I held the bloodied tail in my hand, the owner of which would surely now die, and I remembered my manners again. I curtsied and spoke my first Russian word to a Russian soldier. The word was 'thank you' (Спасибо). Who knows, maybe this Russian soldier had a little girl of his own at home.

It was dark when we left. Not knowing where we were it took us a while before we found a farmhouse which must have been somewhere on the outskirts of Rhenitz. The doors were barricaded; we shouted we were Germans looking for shelter. A lone woman opened the doors and we walked in as you did in those days, the house was warm and whatever food was in the cellar was brought up and given to us. We were exhausted and asleep on our feet, I was still upset. On hearing what had happened to us that day, the very kind woman gave me a book. *Don Quichote*. By the light of my own burning piece of lint in a dish of lard I read through the night. I was so grateful for a few hours of peace and comfort. I managed to hang on to this book for quite a few weeks as if it were a talisman, but eventually I was forced to leave it behind somewhere. *Don Quichote* has always been something very special to me.

We were all hunted out of this house the next day, at first hiding in a cellar while marauding soldiers smashed whatever they could lay their hands on. After they had gone we hid again outside in the forest and in the dark sneaked off to find another roof over our heads. We found a place where my mother and uncle cleared the bodies from the inside of the house first; we children were kept waiting outside with my auntie. She had no stomach for bodies. We children were not supposed to know what was going on, but I knew. As days went by fewer and fewer houses were available for shelter, they were all torched by hateful soldiers, who wanted to make sure that no German had anywhere to go. Meeting one minute Russian soldiers who would share their dinner with us and the next those who would happily kill all of us was our own version of Russian roulette. At the same time, amazingly, large numbers of refugees came into our area from the east, from Belarus, the Ukraine and an area from somewhere east of Poland where it used to join Russia. Quite a few could speak reasonable German. Even more surprisingly, Polish soldiers were deserting from the Russian forces; they talked to us, saying that the Russians were no good and as soon as the war with Germany was over, we should join them and fight the Russians. They would do anything to thwart the Russians. We should join them and they would support us. We were utterly confused. 'Wishful thinking of desperate people,' my mother said to me, 'but keep your mouth shut.'

By now we were huddled together in groups of 60 to 100 in a single house, if it had a roof on, just as we had been in our own house until a little while ago. We were constantly molested and harassed by soldiers who acted like animals. Rape became a routine by day and night and all hiding places were carefully explored so that the younger women could disappear within seconds while older women were doing the talking, calming down and appeasing the soldiers and looking after the children. I had a fabulous hiding place, under an improvised settee, so low you would never suspect anyone could fit under there, particularly if people were sitting on it. I desperately had to fight sneezing and coughing attacks, the fluff and dust were so terrible.

One awful night two soldiers dragged a young girl out of her hiding place and her mother implored the soldiers to leave her alone. 'Rather shoot me!' she shouted. Whereupon one soldier said in very good German, 'You want me to shoot you? I will.' And he did. Then they left. The little girl's mother was dead. I felt very sorry for mothers with very young children. They were always found because you cannot tell babies and toddlers to keep quiet. They just cry at the wrong time. Some mothers had their babies killed while they were being raped. Some soldiers must have found crying babies very irritating.

One night a soldier shot another young mother, she struggled too much. She had a little boy. The next morning, a very bleak morning with ice shimmering on the snow, I saw the little boy crawl out of the front door which stood open, he pulled himself up, holding on to a railing by the stairs and he looked so small and vulnerable, he belonged to no one. If he lived, he would never know his name, never know where he came from and would not remember his mummy or daddy, if he was still alive. At that moment I knew unforgiving anger and decided that I would take that soldier's life, he was too much of a danger to all of us.

There was another boy in our group, about my age. He had been picked up by an old couple somewhere in the Ukraine. He had had a nervous breakdown, his parents murdered, he had forgotten his name. So, everyone called him Bubi, little boy. I recognised the soldier who had shot the toddler's mother, he was actually called Ivan. He was known to all of us as a brutal bully and greatly feared. I got Bubi to somehow get Ivan into the barn that day, which was full of straw. There I was waiting, hidden by bales of straw. There was no shortage of weapons of all kinds. A rifle was hidden in the straw. When Ivan entered I shot him. Bubi and I dragged his body farther into the barn and covered it well with straw. I was satisfied. Ivan would not shoot my mother tonight. If the Russians could shoot us, well then, we could shoot them. We could all arm ourselves to the teeth. Weapons were lying about everywhere, mainly taken from dead soldiers. I was at that time neither child nor grown-up, but turned out to be particularly tough and strong in spite of the poor food. I also had the tendency to do my own thing; somehow or other I had to learn to stand on my own feet. Every day I could see women shot and snuffed out as if they were some undesirable insect, no thought was given to their children. I was surrounded by so many helpless orphans. It stood to reason that one day I might have to look after my sister and two brothers on my own.

One Russian soldier even gave me shooting lessons. He was harmless and good natured, he laughed a lot and regarded it as fun. To teach children to shoot was in those times about the equivalent of teaching a child to eat with a knife and fork. The AK47 was not in circulation then, I think the weapon we used for my shooting lessons was the PPSh, which is not as heavy as it looks, but it is damn effective. I believe the rifle which I used in the barn to shoot Ivan was a German weapon, I had seen it so often. You had to be more experienced to hit someone with that rifle. I did not have the experience then, but my target had been almost within reach.

Otherwise I was too puny and thin and unattractive to be of interest to the soldiers and yet, in many ways I became again 'the man of the house'. I was stronger than the German men that were still around, they were old and feeble and no threat to anyone. Boys? If they were my age they better stay in hiding or they would be shot; even the younger ones were in danger. We were back to biblical times, quite a few soldiers saw themselves as King Herods.

The soldiers treated me like a quirky mascot, someone to laugh about, but I acquired skills which could have been quite dangerous in unscrupulous hands. At the same time I had the digestion of a camel and the strength of a horse. I think I was also a quick learner of the Russian language like my mother. All that would help us to survive in the months to come.

Wherever we ended up, my mother took the lead. What she said was done and she was a very able, natural leader. With so many people crowding into so few houses still standing, sleeping arrangements had to be organised. 30 people in 20 square metres? No problem. If you had two tables it was easy. Push them against the wall of a room, children go on top, anyone longer than the tables goes underneath, that is grown-ups or people my size. The others arranged on the floor like sardines. Not comfortable, but closely packed keeps the temperature up. Young women close to the windows with the very old men for a very good reason. My dear little sister would tell stories and fairy tales as always, which kept the other children quiet and was very appreciated by all the others.

My brave mother, dressed up as a very old woman with some kind of ash and dirt as make-up, together with a really old woman, slept by the front door. They did not really sleep, anticipation of what the night might bring kept them alert. They were waiting for the inevitable knock on the door. 'Kto tam?' Then the inevitable palaver in German/Russian to gain time before opening. Both women had considerable persuasive powers, they showed sympathy, motherliness, both had enviable negotiating skills, both were shameless liars. They were overjoyed to see the Russian army, because they had so longed for freedom and would do anything to help the boys and would they bring in their washing next morning, it would be the least they could do for them, gladly.

Young women? Here? No, look for yourself. While the chitchat had been in progress the old men had helped the young women get through the window without making a noise. My courageous uncle always stayed outside to act as a look-out and to make sure their escape route was safe. When the soldiers tried to rush in, they were straight away hampered by the table full of children, more underneath, the odd one had by then started crying. That did not exactly look like an inviting harem. So they left. One did, of course, always have to hope that the odd wild one would not lose his temper and let his anger out on those that were present. That was a chance one had to take. When they had gone, before long, another group would arrive and the whole frightening performance would start all over again. Sleep was a luxury not to be had at night, you snatched a few winks during the day. But they brought their washing the next morning and the washing of their comrades as well. It was an uneasy stand-off, but it held.

The soldiers even organised a big thank you one day. They came along in a big tank, parked in front of the house and called us all outside onto the road. They produced many jars of preserved gooseberries which they had found somewhere, next they syphoned fuel out of the tank, almost two buckets-full were filled with this liquid. The gooseberries were added and this delicious cocktail was distributed to all. Not even the smallest children were overlooked. The soldiers were happy, they drank a lot themselves and saw to it that I got a big tin full of the stuff as well. They patted me and the other children on the head and were clearly very pleased with their good deeds. And so they should have been. I could not help admiring them. There was a war, tempers were fickle, soldiers could rain honey and pitch on to you, but sometimes their good hearts would shine through all adversity and we would relax as if we were among our own. Having tasted the truly breathtaking drink and having swallowed it with a smile under the stern eyes of my mother, I will happily recommend it as a cure for diphtheria.

The soldiers then really got merry; one of them had found an accordion, they made music and sang and danced on the icy road. I had never seen such light-footed, spontaneous, energetic dances, with steps I had not seen before. I was enthusiastic and full of admiration. The steps were not like the Hungarian dances I had learnt from Theresia at school. Later I practised the new steps, they were very hard and gave me wobbly knees. But then, I did not have much food inside me.

All song and merriment came to an end the following night. We met rowdies again. The young women had fled into the barn, but one had been seen running in there and as the soldiers could not find them in the dark, one put a match to the straw. It is in the nature of straw that it catches and spreads very fast. No one got out and half an hour later there were more small orphans to be shared among the remaining women. We hastily left this house and made off to find some other shelter. The fire was bad in many ways. Children had lost their mothers and all of us had lost food. We had some chickens and a milking cow hidden away in that barn. The cinders were too hot to pick over and retrieve the cooked cow.

In our new area we were again acquainted with the barbaric streak in human nature. We lost several old men, beaten to death and another unfortunate woman succumbed to what may have been pneumonia. One of the refugees was a Russian nun. She had been gang raped the night before. She was inconsolable. I found her in the barn near our new house. She looked so sad and depressed. I sat down on the bale of straw next to her. I asked her about her convent and religion, she talked a little about her faith and how heartbroken she was that she could not have saved herself for her bridegroom in heaven, but he would help her and life on earth would get better again.

I should have paid more attention to what she was saying. I cannot blame it entirely on my age. Too young to understand? I am not so sure. I did not listen properly to a grieving person. So, I presented her with my own lack of hope and said, 'Things will never get better again.' I should not have said this because she was truly depressed and despair from a child's mouth is hard to take. I know that now. She gave me a long look and pulled out of her long black dress a silver ring (Tula silver) with a very dark stone surrounded by other small sparkling stones. 'Take this,' she said, 'and whenever you look at it remember to believe in loving kindness.' I thanked her, somewhat surprised, and left the barn. I wore the ring with the stone on the inside of my hand. It fitted well. The nun had had fine fingers.

Back in the house there was pandemonium. Only four young women left and two very old ones, too old to be of any use and more of a liability and, not counting myself, about 22 young children and babies. I and my three siblings still had our mother. One toddler still had his original mother, she was very young and spoke only Russian. What on earth were all the Russian and Polish refugees doing here, living with us? The other little children had no one.

One of the four women was my auntie. The fourth woman, middle-aged, was depressed and of not much help. My mother was just trying to make some sugar water for a baby – there had been a bag of sugar in the house, the baby's mother had already been murdered and the cow had been incinerated, so no milk. Keeping tiny babies alive was almost impossible.

Suddenly the middle-aged woman stood up, started screaming and shouting 'I have had enough, I cannot take any more. I don't care about anything anymore.' She picked up a chair and threw it right against the opposite wall of the room. My mother put the baby down, rushed over to her and grabbed her hard. She punched her, slapped her, knocked her down, pulled her out of the room, along the hall, opened the door and threw her down the outside stairs out of the house. I heard her say, 'I don't mind you losing your nerve, but we have children in this house and while they are here you behave yourself. We don't need your help but unless you can sit in a corner quietly, don't dare to come back in.' And she closed the door with a bang.

After this violent performance all was mousy quiet inside. No one cried or argued. Silence. The babies and small toddlers were fed, washed, cuddled, put down to sleep. Everyone was on automatic, mentally exhausted. And everyone knew, you don't mess with my mother. Her priorities were clear, her method hard and sharp. What would have happened if we had allowed our small, besieged community to be turned into a mad house? For me it was the usual hard work that I had become accustomed to for several years now, my mother's back-up. At least she knew she could rely on me. I tried so hard not to let her down. Go here, go there, fetch this, fetch that. Find some wood for cooking in the barn. I went.

And that is when I saw her. My nun. Dangling from a beam in the barn. I went back to the house. 'The nun has hanged herself.' 'Well, my lovely,' said my mother, 'we are here to look after the living and cannot help her. Get a ladder, cut her down and bury her in the front garden where the bushes are. The ground will be less frozen there.' So I did. It was a shallow grave. I had no strength to dig deep and yes, the ground was less frozen there. I managed to cover her face with the folds of her ample frock without leaving her indecent and, leaning on my spade, I recited a poem for her, *Frühling, ja, Du bist's, Dich hab ich vernommen.* That was on the 3rd of March. I still have the ring.

Frühling läßt sein blaues Band	Spring lets his blue ribbons
Wieder flattern durch die Lüfte.	flutter through the air again.
Süße, wohlbekannte Düfte	Sweet familiar scents
Streifen ahnungsvoll das Land.	drift over the countryside,
Veilchen träumen schon	full of promise;
Wollen balde kommen.	Violets are already dreaming
Horch von Fern,	of their time to come.
ein leiser Harfenton!	Listen; soft sound of a distant harp!
Frühling, ja du bist's!	It must be you, Spring;
Dich hab' ich vernommen.	it is you I have heard.

Back in the house there was a job waiting. My uncle and another rather old man had been out looting, the equivalent of a shopping trip. They had returned with half a bucket full of rye. Dirty and contaminated with chicken droppings, yes, but rye. We found a coffee mill. My job, grind the rye. It took half a night. The resulting so-called flour was mixed with water and baked. The end product was related to bread, not a close relative, more of a distant cousin. It was shared and eaten by all, still hot. The middle-aged woman that my mother had thrown out had come back in, very quietly. The night was routine. Knock on the door. Kto tam? Palaver. My mother never seemed to sleep and grew ever thinner. But she remained alert and quick.

The next day my uncle had to go alone on the shopping trip. The old man, who had already lost his family, had now also lost his will to live. I found him hanging in the barn. Job for me. I dug his grave close to the nun's, where I had already broken the ground the day before. The poem this time was *Und dräut der Winter noch so sehr.* I recited all verses.

Und dräut der Winter noch so sehr
Mit trotzigen Gebärden,
Und streut er Eis und Schnee umher,
Es muß doch Frühling werden.

Und drängen Nebel noch so dicht
Sich vor den Blick der Sonne,
Sie wecket doch mit ihrem Licht
Einmal die Welt zur Wonne.

Blast nur ihr Stürme, blast mit Macht,
Mir soll darob nicht bangen,
Auf leisen Sohlen über Nacht,
Kommt doch der Lenz gegangen.

Da wacht die Erde grünend auf,
Weiß nicht, wie ihr geschehen,
Und lacht in den sonnigen Himmel hinauf,
Und möcht vor Lust vergehen.

Sie flicht sich blühende Kränze ins Haar
Und schmückt sich mit Rosen und Ähren,
Und läßt die Brünnlein rieseln klar,
Als wären es Freudenzähren!

Drum still, und wie es frieren mag,
O Herz, gib dich zufrieden,
Es ist ein großer Maientag
Der ganzen Welt beschieden.

Und wenn dir oft auch bangt und graut,
Als sei die Höll' auf Erden:
Nur unverzagt auf Gott gebaut,
Es muß doch Frühling werden.

And even if winter threatens to go on and on
With sullen gestures,
Scattering ice and snow around,
It must be spring again.

And even if the dense fog pushes itself
Before the rays of the sun,
The sun will reawaken and breathe
pleasantly onto the world again.

Blast you winds, blow with all your might
You do not make me tremble,
With stealthy steps and overnight,
Spring will come again.

The earth will reawaken, verdant,
Not knowing what has come to pass,
And smile up at the sunny sky,
Beside herself with lust for life.

She weaves flower wreaths in her hair
And is adorned with roses and ears of wheat,
Every little fountain can ripple clear
Just like tears of purest joy!

So be still my heart and rest assured
Even if you are still frozen,
It is a perfect day in May
That awaits the entire world.

And if you feel full of dread,
As if there is hell on earth,
Fear not and trust in God,
It will be spring again.

Poetry became connected with death. I had learnt so many poems, but there were so many deaths that in the end I ran out of them and one poem had to serve more than one person, even groups of them. That was the 4th of March.

That night my auntie was raped. My uncle could not help her. He was beaten up. He took it badly, went into the barn and hanged himself. What a sad end for such a compassionate, kind-hearted man, who had helped so many, friend or foe, risking his own life under the Nazis. My mother tried to comfort my auntie while I buried my uncle close to the other two graves. An old man walked by and when he heard my spade crunch in the crisp ice on the frozen ground, he came round the hedge and when he saw what I was doing, he took off his hat and recited something from the Bible that I did not know. I left it like that. To add something else would be like gilding the lily. But I thanked my uncle for the many presents he had given me and remembered how kindly he had always selected the best apples from the tree to give to me. The sun used to sparkle on his gold-rimmed glasses in his beloved, well-kept garden. It was a hard farewell for me. That was on the 5th. My mother was touched by this loss in more than one way. We had no one to go foraging any more, a problem that was solved in the next few days. But first to the next morning.

My auntie was missing. 'Go and find her,' said my mother. We knew what we were looking for. And, as I went I kept looking up. I looked in the barn, nothing. I went to nearby trees, nothing. She could not have gone far. So, back to the house, look in the loft. And I found her there. I opened the attic door and stopped on the top of the stairs. My heart seemed to stop, too. My dearest, kindest, happy auntie was kneeling before me, her body held up by the rope round her neck. She looked so alive and how did she hang herself kneeling? I did get so frightened and could barely suppress my tears. But there was no time to lose. The other children would be around soon and I had to get her body out of the house. It was hard work. I kept saying sorry, sorry in case I hurt her as I dragged her body bump-bump down the stairs, at the bottom a quick look down the hall, no one about, then out of the door and into the front garden. I eventually managed to place her into her pitifully shallow grave and then I faced a dilemma. What to cover her face with? She was still wearing her glasses. She would not need them any more. Glasses were valuable, they could be bartered, perhaps for food. But I did not have the heart to remove them. And a thought occurred to me. I am really a poorly specimen, not suited for survival in times like this. Apart from feeling sorry for myself for this shortcoming, I could do nothing about it. I could not change myself, so I buried my auntie with glasses. I experienced real grief. I remembered the many songs she had sung for me and taught me. Now it was my turn to sing to her. I sang H. Heine's *wenn Du eine Schwalbe siehst, sag, ich laß sie grüßen.* The original wording is wenn *Du eine Rose schaust.* That was the 6th.

Sag' ihr, ich laß sie grüßen,
Sag' ihr, es geht mir gut.
Sprich nicht von den Tränen
Und wie weh mein Herz noch tut ...

Sag' ihr, ich laß sie grüßen,
Sag' ihr, ich bin vergnügt.
Sprich nicht von der Hoffnung,
Die so oft mein Herz belügt ...

Grüß sie, wenn du sie siehst
Und wenn sie dann von mir spricht.
Erzähl' ihr das, was du willst,
Nur die Wahrheit,
Die sag' bitte, bitte nicht! – oh-oh-oh

Sag' ihr, ich laß sie grüßen,
Sag' ihr, es geht mir gut.
Sie ging fort, fort von mir.
Und sie weiß, daß nichts mir blieb.
Trotzdem sag' ihr: Ich hab' sie lieb.

Sag' ihr, ich laß sie grüßen,
Sag' ihr, es geht mir gut.
Sie ging fort, fort von mir,
Und sie weiß, daß nichts mir blieb.
Trotzdem sag' ihr: Ich hab' sie lieb.

Ich hab' sie lieb

I am not sure how accurate this translation is:

Tell her I said hello, tell her I'm fine
Don't talk of the tears and how my heart still hurts

Tell her I said hello, tell her I'm happy
Don't talk of the hope that lies to my heart

Say hello when you see her and when she talks of me
Tell her what you like but not the truth
Please, please don't tell her that

Tell her I said hello, tell her I'm fine
She went away, away from me
And she knows there's nothing left for me
Tell her anyway, I love her so

Tell her I said hello, tell her I'm fine
She went away, away from me
And she knows there's nothing left for me
Tell her anyway, I love her so
I love her so.

Within a few short weeks, only five, I was worlds away from my previous life, but thanks to my open-minded, intelligent, caring, warmhearted and tolerant upbringing in early life, I had basically learnt that all people are the same. There are some fine nuances:

some are like this, some are like that; and then there is a third group, they are quite different. You may not like some of them. Don't worry, the ones you don't like may not like you either. But you must make an effort to live with and accept them all. You must accept responsibility for your fellow human beings and help those who are weak. It may be no more than taking extra sandwiches to school to give to someone who would otherwise go hungry. Do not expect praise for such a natural gesture.

From the beginning of March we saw an ominous development. Large herds of cows, sheep and horses were being driven along the main road leading east. Occupied Germany was systematically plundered. Any animals fit to walk or at least capable of stumbling on for just a few kilometres were herded together and set on the road to Russia. It was a pitiful sight. They were bony with open wounds, limping on injured legs, hungry, thirsty, whipped and beaten and they looked close to death. Few would have made it to Russia. They became pointless victims of the war. They were useless to the Poles and Russians if they were meant to be reparations because they probably died before they got to their destination. They were useless to us, we were not allowed to have them; food was not meant to be for us Germans. It was a tragedy for the entire area east of the Oder and in some parts even west of the river the country was stripped of all livestock. If it could not walk it was killed anyway, at least it could not be of any use to a German. The idea was to deprive us of any source of food. And it worked. Death from starvation was commonplace. Although the order was violence, cold, with starvation a close third. We had lived with an acute shortage of food for a long time and the arrival of the Russian army had accelerated this process. The thousands lying dead by the wayside were testimony to the consequences of war.

Dead animals lying in the road were of no use to us either. When did they die? How long ago? You do not touch dead meat. Some did. That reduced the numbers of survivors further. Neither do you eat ice or snow. You may well be suffering from hunger and thirst but with a bit of luck you would still be alive tomorrow, and tomorrow you may find a little food or drink. But eat a dead carcass or drink unboiled snow or ice and you may never see tomorrow. For tomorrow's survivors, of course, the dead were a bonus because if food did turn up the next day there were fewer left to eat it. You can only be alive tomorrow if you can survive today.

What was needed was a freshly killed animal. So my mother took the risk of talking to the drovers. They were, as a rule, German women forced to accompany the herds supervised by heavily armed soldiers. My mother had the gift of asking the right soldiers: they had to be the ones at the back of the herds and their faces had to look right. You only had to find such a person every third or fourth day. Such a person would then shoot an animal and walk on as if nothing had happened. The soldiers were forbidden to do so of course, but my mother reckoned some would be like Daddy; and they were. You just had to pick the right one. That shot animal would then vanish fast. We were in the habit of eating everything that came our way immediately and we stuffed as much as possible inside ourselves, not knowing where and when the next meal would come from. My mother led a risky life. Her life hung by a thread made of two intertwining strands. One was despair, the other daring. She always got it right.

It was not only the animals that went east. Day after day there were convoys of lorries loaded high with chairs, buckets, plates, beds, clothing, tools, cupboards, curtain rails, pots, you name it, it was on the lorries. The contents of the entire area east of the Oder vanished farther east; a huge section of a country completely stripped of everything movable that was of value. If it was not nailed to the ground, it was taken and millions of people were left destitute, bewildered, starving and dying.

We changed our hideouts to various houses in that area, still somewhere within a few kilometres of Rhenitz. Sometimes we went back to places we had been in before; it was not safe to stay in just one place, close to a main road where Russian troops were still moving west or where they themselves were occupying houses for a few hours or a whole day before driving on. The refugees we were with constantly changed. The mainly young women formed quickly into supportive little groups, irrespective of nationality and never mind what language they spoke. We were never short of Polish or Russian mothers and we were so glad, as they could act as interpreters. The women were far outnumbered by lost or orphaned little children.

Thinking back on this time, I am still deeply touched by the loving care which these mothers showed for all children. Some women had lost all of their own. I remember one in particular. Once she had had four children but her husband was in the Party. You were in it sometimes even if you had not applied for membership. Your identity card arrived and that was that. You may not even have known that you were in it, if your identity card was not sent. Don't tell me I am fantasising. It is true. Someone will be able to corroborate what I am claiming. During the first few days in February 1945 the Russians succeeded in seeking out most Party members and shot all of them and their families, as was done to my friends, Irene and Ingeborg, and whoever happened to be in the same house with them at the time. In the case of this lovely woman, they shot her husband, all four children, including a ten-day old baby, and set fire to their house. They let her live as punishment. No matter how hard I try to understand the reason for the perpetrators' actions I have never to this day been able to figure it out. How could these two-legged creatures not see the futility of their actions? In their zeal to teach others a lesson they overlooked the fact that now that their victims were dead, they could no longer learn.

After the murder of her family this good woman ran out into the whiteness quite demented. As she ran past a dead woman in the snow, she heard a baby cry. The mother had been shot, but her baby lying under her was alive. She rescued the baby and by the time we got to know her, she had picked up a total of seven children. She treated them like her own. None of them knew their names, they were too small and some of the older ones had more or less suffered a nervous breakdown and could not remember anything, like Bubi.

There were some people who prayed to God and thanked him for saving the seven children whom he had protected and saved in his goodness. I became aware of that very rebellious streak in me. Were there any siblings? How many? Where were they now? Were they still alive? Where was God when the children's parents were killed? His divine arithmetic did not add up. We knew of four children plus seven, that makes eleven children in my reckoning. But there were only seven. And if I should end up in heaven, which I will, because by the time I die, hell will be so overcrowded that the devil will not have room for any more sinners, God will most likely forgive me for my sins. I will tell him: don't bother God, because I will *never* forgive you. I have so far not seen any reason to change my mind.

There was something very eerie about my mother. She seemed to have a sixth sense. The sense of danger. Once we tried for shelter in a farmhouse that had a well inside the kitchen, a *Brunnen*. We were just about to have a drink of water when she suddenly panicked and shouted: 'Get out, get out!' As I was not fast enough she kicked me hard and with her arms full with my little brothers and my sister clinging to me, we made it out of the house and across the yard. As we reached the gate a bomb flattened the house completely and we were swept off our feet. It was a direct hit. We had not heard the plane coming. The aim of bombers was poor in those days, but if you drop enough bombs, one of them will get you eventually and you die only once.

On another occasion we took shelter in woodland and were so glad not to be seen from the open road. We could rest. There was even a bench on which to sit. And again in a real frenzy my mother suddenly kicked us off the bench and hurried us well away from it. Within seconds a hand grenade exploded under the bench. We all trembled, white-faced with fear. My mother murmured: to find woodland with a bench to sit on is too good to be true, something will be wrong. One should not push one's luck. We had become a very mistrusting little family.

It was near that very woodland that a large group of soldiers, several hundred, came marching along. They were German POWs guarded by Russian soldiers. The contrast between the Russians and the Germans was heartbreaking. The Russians were fully grown men. The Germans were mere boys, perhaps 16 years old or so, like the brothers of my school friends. The boys themselves pretended to be cheerful, made thumbs up signs, even shouted not to worry and, yes, they had enough to eat. They all marched off in the direction of Soldin. Well, even if they had enough to eat it would do them no good. I found out a little later they never reached Soldin. Somehow I never left that terrifying road littered with the evil deeds of man. It was only about six kilometres long. I remember the other stretch of road I had walked, from my town to Soldin, about 30 kilometres on 13 February. How much bestiality had I witnessed on just two roads in two days? And how many roads were there, east of the Oder? I am not swayed by post-war statistics that give the numbers of those that died (or rather, were murdered) in that part of Europe during the first five months of 1945 as perhaps a million point something something. No, let me say it, many millions, five, six, seven? No one can put sand into my eyes. I have seen what I have seen. The bodies were piled up by the roadside by the thousand, and I buried them by the hundred.

My mother and I had been very worried about the fate of my grandmother left behind in Soldin. I could be trusted to stay in hiding somewhere for 48 hours. But my brothers and my sister? Then we found an ideal place. A burnt-out house with burnt out-buildings, part of which had collapsed, forming a nice little hideaway like a large dog house. All four of us children fitted in there. We climbed in with a supply of parboiled swedes and promised to keep mousy quiet until my mother got back. She left that night.

It was a dangerous undertaking. She could not use the main road. She arrived in Soldin in the morning and cautiously found her way back to the rubble of the house where we had left grandmother. There was no one to ask. The town was deserted and if anyone was there, they stayed out of sight. Amazingly, the kindhearted woman who had offered us shelter that first night in Soldin was still alive and the news about my grandmother was good. She had recovered and had only just left. She had decided to go back to our own house. Her reasoning was that if any one of us were to survive our ordeal we would eventually go home. In those days people would leave messages written on the walls of their houses, to say where they had been, where they were going, with whom and when. Exact dates could no longer be given as everyone seemed to have lost track of time, but what a relief it was if you found a message from a beloved person, obviously still alive on that day.

We really lived like animals. The females would hide their young when they went out to find food or a better location. We tried, of course, to move back into houses. The climate in the east in early spring is unforgivably cold and without shelter, deadly. Inside a house you could cook better than outside, one could even have a wash. The work was shared among the few women that had come together. Most of them always acted as look-outs, the slightest sign of a Russian vehicle about and we would all melt away, sometimes into the most uncomfortable and quite filthy holes. We noticed that Russian troop movements had slowed down. Instead of driving through, quite a few groups would stop for a while in certain places. That was dangerous for us. There were always marauding groups searching for women, at night of course, as the soldiers were kept busy during the day. But at night they left no house unsearched and no stone unturned.

In the evenings the children would be hidden and by now they were well trained. Under no circumstances utter a sound, crying will not get your mummy back, only silence. There were few babies about now, most had died. The rest of us, including me, would stay outside at vantage points with a good view all round, always alert and ready to scamper away, sometimes far away from where the younger children were hidden. Once we were caught in searchlights mounted on a vehicle. What a fright. My mother remembered a dip alongside a road. We all dived into it and out of reach of the lights we crawled along the bottom of the dip towards a stream. My mother reckoned that they would not look for us in a stream. The snow and ice had partially melted so we left no tracks.

We watched as the soldiers arrived at the spot where we had been sighted. They gave up and turned away. But we had nowhere to go and had no other choice but to stay for the rest of the night where we were. That meant clinging to the willow branches close to and partially in the water, still covered in places with broken ice. I was not the only one suffering from exposure and mortal fear. I went into a repetitive and automatic mode. Trembling all over I repeated again and again in a very low and staccato voice the words from Geoethe's *Dr Faust*: *Osterspaziergang*, '*Vom Eise befreit sind Strom und Bäche*' ('released from their ice are rivers and brooks'). I was unable to do or say anything else. I felt more than half dead when we left our hellish hideout in the morning. Anyone with a frail disposition would not have survived February and March 1945. Where there had been perhaps 500 of us a few weeks ago, there were now probably only 100 left, the dead were still lying by the roadside, unburied. So far in my short life I had learned that living creatures multiply. Now the dead, who can do nothing, multiplied. My mind acknowledged it with a shiver. The dead could not be buried. The ground was frozen, there was no one there with the time or energy to bury them and no tools.

So, inevitably, there were mountains of bodies about. It was no good thinking 'I cannot take any more of this.' If you wanted to live, you looked at the dead with fear and cringed, yes, but then you had to put one foot in front of the other and 'walk on, child, walk on.' The ones that didn't joined the dead.

And yet, even when we seemed utterly useless to each other, we could be useful to some other human being. One night a young Polish soldier stumbled into our midst. He was utterly distraught, shaking and crying. Whatever had happened to him? Trembling, he pointed to his badly torn pullover. He wanted it mended. My mother made cooing noises, got the garment off him, got him hot water and coaxed him to sleep. The pullover was beyond repair. We rummaged through the house and found the former occupant's knitting needles, then we unravelled the torn garment and both of us started knitting. Just as well I had been taught to knit. Out of odds and ends and knitting through the night we produced a front and back and stitched it on to the young soldier while he was anxiously standing there waiting to get away in the morning. Still terrified, he communicated his thanks. I wonder what caused his strange behaviour; and did he make it to the other side of 1945?

I myself nearly did not make it. There were two occasions when I was very close to being snuffed out. This was one of them. Because of my extreme concentration on staying alive the circumstances that led to this situation are blotted out in my memory. I was in a group of people that were sprayed with bullets, as was routine in those days. If it was German, you shot it. But I got away. I remember running but coming to a stop somewhere. The road ended, I turned round and saw a soldier coming towards me. I don't remember the background of the figure. Was there any green? Bushes? Trees? A shed? Buildings? Anything? I don't remember. Was there a sky? Was it blue? Was it grey? Did the sun shine? I don't know. I only saw the figure. Nothing else. I knew I must concentrate on that figure. I did. It was a Mongolian face that came nearer. The face was full of hate. The figure put a hand out for me. Perhaps no more than four steps away. I had a weapon in my hands. It was heavy. I pulled the trigger. The bullet went through the figure's right hand. The figure stopped moving. The face showed surprise. He turned his hand towards his face. The back of his hand was now turned to me. I saw a bluish/black mark in the middle of his right hand. Black-red drops of blood were running down his wrist. The world had become totally silent, it was far away. Eternity was touchable. Only seconds could have passed. But I had time to analyse every fraction of a second. I had time to think about the pros and cons of my desperate situation and the figure's situation. I remember thinking:

I did not ask you to be here.
You did not want to be here.
I did not want to be here.
But life has thrown us together.
But both of us cannot now stay alive.
Only one of us can get out of this alive.
You are trying to kill me.

I do not want to kill anyone, not even you.

But now I have to, because out of the two of us I am the better person. I deserve to live. So I will kill you.

The bloodied hand moved away from his face. Pure hate, the lust for revenge were engraved on his features. I calmly raised the weapon again. I felt ice cool. I allowed the face to come as close to me as was safe. I knew what I was going to do. I knew I would not miss. I pulled the trigger for a second time. Without hearing the sound of the shot I saw a bluish/grey mark appear below his right eye and the face disappeared. I then remember running, running. I lived. I believe the weapon was a Luger.

 I had come a long way. It was only two or three weeks before that I had believed that I was a poorly specimen not suited for survival in times like this.

HOME

My mother judged that I was now grown up and could hold my own and therefore responsible enough to take on the serious duty of looking after a vulnerable person; her mother, about 40 or so kilometres away alone at home, who did not even know that we were still alive. So, my sister and two brothers were left with a young Ukrainian mother and the two of us set off at night for the long march back home.

Oh, how my homeland looked. What devastation, ghostly ruins, well known but now almost unrecognisable landmarks. The smell of burning, of soot, the stench of unburied bodies. The 'walk on, child' had become second nature to me and I bravely moved on like a mechanical doll without showing any emotion. The last bit was the easy bit, because there was no emotion left in any of us. The desire to stay alive drove us on. What a relief, at the end of our exhaust-ing walk, as we stumbled through our front door and made for the secret cellar and called my grandmother's name. She emerged from the darkened hole, unbelievably thin; could anyone still be alive looking like this? We remained silent, almost composed, just hugged each other, no tears, taking in the overwhelming feeling of joy that we were alive. What an unexpected gift.

Urgent news was exchanged, my mother explained why we had come, I was to stay and look after my grandmother and I knew where the preserving jars were buried. Food for the immediate future was assured and my mother would come back with the other children as soon as it was safe. No sign of my great-grandfather. After a short rest, more hugs and kisses, my mother took off again on her perilous journey back to Rhenitz where we later knew she arrived after only 40 hours absence; a superhuman achievement for a person without food. She had left her emergency ration with her mother and me.

So, there I was. Home again. And what a homecoming that was. Home was the secret cellar, my grandmother had furnished it with straw, that was it. There were no blankets, no cushions, no spare clothing, only what we wore. No plate, no pot, no cup, cutlery, candle, no fire, nothing. But my grandmother and I always had an oval German army issue aluminium pot on a string tied round our waist. It was our standard equipment and, of course, a pocket knife. Never be without one. We had no fire, so we could not cook. But what a lucky coincidence, we had no food. We had nothing that needed cooking. So that was one worry we did not have.

I searched the outbuildings, sheds, barn, workshops – we also once had a generously equipped carpenter's shop, because a large property always needs repairs – I found nothing of any use, every bit of machinery, every tool, every nail, every spade, fork, ladder, every piece of wire or wood had gone. Even the large cauldrons in the utility kitchen were ripped out. What was not taken was destroyed.

Then I remembered we had left some tools in our bomb shelter, in case we had to dig ourselves out. As there was no soul about to see me I searched the bunker, clearing the entrance with my hands and sure enough, I found what I needed – some spades and fire-making equipment. I took a spade, covered the other tools with sand and started digging where I had hidden the jars of preserves given to me by my auntie, who I had only recently buried. I unearthed some pears and plums and one jar contained glucose powder. I covered the rest and prepared to run with this precious food back to the house where my grandmother was waiting.

It was only when I looked about that I became aware of the vast emptiness around me. Theoretically I was in our orchard. Was I? Where was the orchard? The orchard had gone, only broken twigs, scattered. No cherries, no apples, no plums, no pears, no peaches, no apricots. Of one type of plum tree alone, the Hausmanns Zwetschke, we had 51 of them. They made almost black, delicious *Pflaumenmus* (plum compote). Now there was only wilderness. The two fully grown walnut trees, gone. I looked beyond the house where I always enjoyed the singing of the starlings early in the morning in spring. There were no starlings, the huge birch that held their nests, gone. The mature horse chestnut and pear trees around the house, gone. The grapevines that had covered the east, south and west sides of the house were sawn through just above ground. I dared to turn my head and raised my eyes. Where was the forest at the far end of our fields? A stand of majestic 120-year-old Scots pine, gone. The *Schonung* (tree nursery) with sections of 20- and 40-year-old pines, gone. As far as I could see there was emptiness, devastation, the burnt-out ruins of the forester's house and that of a tenant farmer could now be glimpsed; before they had been hidden from view by the trees.

I rushed with my jars back to the house, put them on the floor and ran through all the rooms of my birthplace. Empty rooms, bare walls, not one stitch of anything that had once been there. Not down-stairs, upstairs, in the attic rooms, not in the loft. My own room? Torn books, broken pencils, ruined watercolours, oil colours, a smashed guitar, mandolin, violin. And then my doll. There she was, still beautiful. But who had undressed my doll? Her clothes were taken. She was naked. My skin crawled, I slammed the door and ran back to my grandmother who was opening the jars of fruit. I must have looked upset. She said: 'I am so sad you have to see your home like this.' But I felt suddenly quite protective towards her and assured her: 'Not to worry, after the war we will build it all up again.' I was such an ignoramus. Now what I had so recently seen on the roads was perfectly explained. The hundreds and hundreds of lorries going past us east loaded to the brim with household goods, machinery, wood and everything that was removable made sense, a country ransacked, even the forests gone. How was anyone to survive? If you were German you were not meant to survive and most didn't. I did. I was there.

My town had a large lake, 30 metres deep. There was little access all round because of its narrow ledge. A very small part of the lake was used for public bathing with heavy beams anchored 6–8m away from the sandy edge with a warning: 'Only swimmers beyond this point.'

At this time when I had been taken back to my town to look after my grandmother, Russian soldiers had marched a large number of German civilians in the direction of Küstrin on their way to be 'resettled' in the west. The civilians were made up of women and children. Men were at this stage in short supply, they were already dead, regardless of their age.

When these poor people reached the lake they were beaten senseless by the soldiers and thrown into the water. Any that showed signs of life and tried to get out of the lake were pushed back in. There were no survivors.

Later, after my mother had collected me and taken me back to the Rhenitz area again, the few surviving members of my cousin's family made their way back to the town. I know from my cousin's letters that the stench in the town was quite unbearable. In cold waters bodies decompose slowly, they float on top, presenting a terrifying, heartbreaking sight. She wrote they were plagued by swarms of flies.

Her family and the people who were with them were struck down by typhus. My little cousin, who was then nine years old, was the only one to care for all of them and in due course nursed almost all of them to death. Her sister, a few years older, survived the disease. The little girl herself did not get it. Typhus has its carriers. As I mentioned earlier, she survived the war and she wrote to me a few short years ago that she had also started to record the events of

1945, but she wrote: 'I could not continue. I just could not get past the Soldiner Chaussee.' Dear cousin, I could not have done it either, without escaping into another language.

Again, our relationship with our POWs had come into play. When 'their' Pole heard that the Germans were to be expelled the next day (the Germans themselves were not informed) he had come round to them at night, secretly, and taken them into a bombed-out building and also smuggled food into their hiding place at night. Jucek, that was his name, did this because he did not think that they would survive the forced march to Küstrin in their weakened state. With his help they managed to survive until it was safe to show themselves again. They were then thrown out of their homeland with the second wave of expulsions.

Next: where was great-grandfather? At first I was not told, but the truth could not be hidden. Shortly after we had left our home on 13 February with only the very old and sick left behind unable to follow their families, Russian trucks had pulled up. The soldiers collected all the stranded people and loaded them onto their vehicles. Great-grandfather had been badly beaten; he seemed to have gone to sleep after we had left and had not heard the soldiers' knock on the door. That was according to a woman who had taken refuge in our house and was lucky enough to evade the soldiers. The old people were driven to what we called 'the little mill'. They were beaten and, unable to help themselves, were barricaded in and the little mill set on fire. An old man who had managed to escape told us. He had returned to town to tell the story. There were not many left to hear it. But a few brave people made their way to the little mill and, indeed, found it burnt out with bodies inside and the badly burnt corpses of some who had tried to get away to save themselves but never made it close by.

So ended the life of an intelligent, loving man to whom respect for others was as natural as breathing. I am so indebted to him and so thankful that he had been part of my life. I feel I have never done him justice by allowing myself to mourn him, as was his due. I was the last of our family to see him alive, but by the time I learnt of his death, I was living in a glasshouse – I saw, I observed, I pushed it aside, I bypassed it. It got in my way. I had to get on with the business of staying alive. Later, yes, much later on, definitely, I would think about it, put it all into perspective and come to terms with his death, with the deaths of other members of my family, with the deaths of all the others that I never even knew in life. I only knew their bodies, many of which I buried myself. And there was no one I could discuss all this with.

So I turned my attention to immediate needs. Dig up the carrots and swedes which I had squirrelled away in autumn. Then on second thoughts dig some of them back in again; we did not have enough wood to cook them with, fire was strictly rationed and eating them raw seemed like a waste. Find the jars with the currants, the cherries, the rhubarb. I was thankful to my dearest aunt, who advised me to hide this good food and sugar. It was a life saver. I needed wood, dry wood, to make a fire with. So I roamed my home area and met five other children, equally deprived, destitute, thin and big-eyed, taking their chances. We did not speak to each other, each word was a waste of energy. We stayed together as a group, like feral cats, perhaps for safety. We followed Russian soldiers at a safe distance. Surely, they did not live on thin air, there must be a food distribution place somewhere. This had to be found.

We found it. It was a field kitchen behind a large building. According to the smoke and smell there was food and fire. We were like bees at the smell of nectar. We waited together along the short road that led to the back of the building. Soldiers stooped, wrapped in big coats, trudged along the path and returned with tins of some sort of food; it smelt heavenly, like stinking boiled cabbage. They returned on the same path with their eyes downcast as they walked past us. They possibly felt guilty with their tins full of hot, steaming squelch that passed as food. One woman soldier walked past us and flung what may have been a piece of bread on the ground before us. She looked at us and put her heel onto it and crunched it into the ground rendering it inedible. We did not react. We knew it was not meant for us, we were not to have it. Not a single crumb. Later on in life I put her behaviour towards us down to people being brain-washed with the idea of collective guilt. We were German children and we deserved what was coming to us. We needed to be punished because we were guilty. Guilty of what? Crimes that we would not have been able to conjure up in our wildest dreams. Collective guilt does not exist in real life. People who support the idea have their own wicked agenda. They are short-sighted, hateful creatures with murderous tendencies, hypocrites. And in years to come I found there are enough stupid people about who worship these monsters as their messiahs.

We children were, by now, used to such displays of pointless cruelty. We would not bother to shrug our shoulders or bat an eyelid. Food was not yours until it was inside you. Then, one soldier, after a quick glance around, passed me a piece of bread, an ender, hard and clearly mouldy, but it had been his and was of great value to him. Perhaps he was thinking of children he had at home. He gave me his bread. I accepted it quickly and quietly. I knew he could not be seen to fraternise with his enemies and he walked away quickly. I left the queue. Once one was given some food, one had no right to stay any longer and wait for more offerings. If there were more gifts to be given, then these gifts were to be received by someone who had had nothing so far.

As I ran away with my precious morsel, I suddenly thought about my best friend Lizzy. Instead of going back to my grandmother I walked towards the house of my friend. It was a long way. The house was still there. I walked into the yard and through the front door. The house was empty, stripped of every piece of furnishing like all the other houses still standing, empty shells, the kitchen empty, bare walls, strange and frightening. I walked on into the parents' bedroom, nothing there, a painting on the wall opposite the door which I had so loved, gone. There was a rustling sound on the floor behind the door. On a bed of straw with a wooden crate next to it and a tin of water on top, I saw my childhood companion, my Lizzy; a kind of ghost, clearly close to dying. She was fighting for breath. I talked to her. She recognised me. I gave up my piece of bread for her. I put it on her bedside 'locker'. She smiled. I said I would go looking for her elder sister to help her eat it. She smiled. I left the room. Something stopped me from touching her or getting close to her. I left the house.

Her sister was not in the house. I stepped into the yard. What to do now? Then I heard the now so familiar clink of a spade on frozen ground behind the barn. I knew what was up. I walked into the barn and, surprisingly, found a spade. I took it and walked round the back of the barn. I saw what I expected to see. Lizzy's sister, only 12 years of age, trying to excavate a hole under the dead rhubarb leaves. The ground under the leaves was less frozen than elsewhere. The wrapped shape in a blanket lying nearby was clearly their mother. I spoke not a word. I silently helped to dig the grave. Again, it was pitifully shallow. The rough mound nearby indicated where Lizzy's little brother had been buried a day earlier.

We placed Lizzy's mother into the grave and closed it. We were exhausted. And still leaning on our spades to recover, Lizzy's sister said, 'It is so sad, I always wanted to be a midwife.' I said, after a pause, 'I left a piece of bread with her, for after.' Meaning when Lizzy was dead, her sister could have it. Funeral service done. Disjointed conversation. Fractured minds.

Lizzy died the same day. She was not buried by her loving sister. Her sister never got to eat the bread. She died less than 24 hours later. Someone found both of them dead in the house the next day. In times of war, cold and hunger, diseases do their rounds, well known killers, not normally associated with daily life. Diphtheria and typhus descended in early 1945. And they will put an end to life in under 24 hours, guaranteed. It was diphtheria that had put an end to my friend's family. Some instinct had told me not to touch and not to go near.

Their father had been requisitioned by the Russian army in early February 1945 to help clear an airfield. To be press-ganged was common practice in any war, presumably still is today. Soldiers have their jobs to do, all other jobs were done by 'you, you and you, get onto that lorry' and off you went. No one was asked, no family members informed, no one knew where you had gone. Perhaps you were shot at the end, perhaps you were released, perhaps you died on the job. Things don't seem to change, they have not changed over many centuries. The Romans called these workers slaves, as did other earlier 'civilisations'. In 1945 they were POWs or forced labour. When Lizzy's father was released, his family was dead. He died a few days later. And that had been the fate that had befallen all my friends and their families. Not one of them had survived. There had been my auburn Ingeborg, my blonde Ingeborg, my Irene and my Lizzy. Now there was just me. And here I am. Reporting their deaths and the deaths of their families. I still record the birthdays of my childhood friends in my annual diaries.

I was then thoroughly depressed. There was no hope. No ray of light. I went round a few houses of former friends and neighbouring properties that were still standing. Most were destroyed, bombed out, burnt. All houses were completely looted, what could not have been taken away, smashed. One room in a large house still had a large wardrobe in it. Curious, I opened it. It contained a decomposed body. I was not shocked or surprised. I closed the wardrobe again. It explained why the wardrobe was still there. I knew that a lot of people had taken poisons, painkillers, sleeping pills and then had hidden away somewhere hoping to die quietly. That is what had happened to this unfortunate person. Just one of so many. And I noted it without any emotion. Was it Stalin who said: 'A single death is a tragedy, a million deaths is a statistic'?

Where had all the people gone? My grandmother and I seemed to be the only living creatures about, plus the odd child near the Russian field kitchen. One day our fire had gone out. I took my heart in both hands and approached the soldiers for fire. I got it. I took it home and we relit grandmother's stove. I had also found in someone's barn an aluminium pot, very battered but which could be kept upright on stones in the fire. And no holes. Now we could boil the swedes and carrots that I had reburied. I found, to my utter delight, grandfather's Goethe, in tatters, in great-grandfather's cellar. It was like a greeting from the past, a reminder of what life was all about and could be so again. A lifeline. I managed to cling to this book against all odds. It became my life support system and I still have it today.

We had the odd visitors, sole survivors of families. They were look-ing for anyone still alive who might be able to tell them something about their missing relatives. Their accounts of what had happened to them since February 1945 were so harrowing that I will not repeat them. I have already said more than enough about what had happened to all of us. Then two unusual visitors came looking for us. They knew we were related to the people they were looking for and they knew where we lived. One was a former POW who had worked for my uncle, who had secretly given his POWs glucose tab-lets and dinners in his kitchen with my aunt. This POW had come back from Holland into the Russian-occupied area to look for my uncle and aunt. Their kindness unforgotten, he wanted to take them back to Holland to help them with a new life. I had by then buried both of them. This POW had a special pass and under the 'protec-tion' of the Russian army could travel back into the war zone.

The other visitor was a French POW, the secret fiancé of my moth-er's cousin. He had found the house of our relatives burnt out and a surviving neighbour had told him the entire family had perished. We knew nothing about them either. Another tragedy. Much later, when André had married in France, they learned of one another's existence again. Life can be so cruel.

Yes, I was back home but I could have been on another planet. Relatives and friends gone. Most had died a fearful death. I pon-dered why, not for the first time. I found no answer. Even animals I was fond of were now dead. In our barn I found the furry remains of our rabbits. With great-grandfather gone so suddenly, there had been no one there even to let them out. The dear little creatures had died of starvation. I buried their furs and bones. Would I have to bury everything that my heart was attached to? My position was really not any better than that of the rabbits. I was becoming morose. I started talking to myself, I recited poem after poem. I was fortunate I knew so many and it stopped me from thinking. The world around me was in such a menacing state and I was incapable of even finding a starting point from which to organise my thoughts into something constructive. I had no hope. But I had my poems and my dancing.

At least I was able, mentally and physically, to overcome the enormous stress I was under.

I visited the patch of ground under the apple tree, where once so long ago I had become aware of the wonder of spring, the joyous corner in the garden where the goslings had invaded my Goethe. I did not cry, I just did not now how to any more. I ran off to my own little garden with the little tree I had grafted under the watchful eyes of my grandfather. And the tree was there. It had escaped all vandalism and destruction. It was alive. It was like discovering life itself again. I remembered another tree that was dear to me. I ran to find it. On the slope at the end of our fields leading to the pine forest that had now gone, there had stood a little pine tree which I had once damaged with my sledge going downhill so fast. I had apologised to the tree and had propped it up again with a branch. Pine trees are so supple when they are young. To my utter delight the tree was still standing there and I danced around it and talked to it and wished it a long life. That was the last I would ever see of my trees. I did not know it but it was my farewell to the forest forever.

I ran home to grandmother. My worried mother had arrived. She had heard that diphtheria was around in our area. I was to go back with her immediately. My grandmother agreed. She would hold the fort. She had fire, a pot, a safe hiding place, swedes, carrots, preserves and when the diphtheria outbreak was over – that would be when no one was left to be killed – my mother would come back with all of us, because somehow a new start had to be made when the war was over. That night we were off on another one of those fearful, merciless marches over uneven ground, 40 kilometres of it. Instead of food I clutched my Goethe.

We found my sister and two brothers well in the care of a Polish mother who had already lost two of her young children, one was still alive. I remember her as a most beautiful woman, but with the big frightened eyes of a child. Thinking back everyone looked jumpy, barely containing their fears. Only my mother had an aura of authority about her, a born matriarch. Whatever she requested was done and everyone had the feeling that her orders made sense and that it was for the best.

Food, which had always been desperately short, existed now virtually only in our fantasies. Whatever had been hidden away had by now been found by someone and eaten. There were no chickens, no pigs, no rabbits, no cows, no cats, no dogs, no pigeons. No potatoes, carrots, swedes, onions, no cabbages, it was too early for spring grasses to grow, no nettles, no sorrel, no dandelions and the dying from starvation began in earnest. It was pointless asking the soldiers for food, their diet consisted of boiled stinking onions, or swedes, or cabbage. They had some bread, it was always mouldy. You had to be virtually immune to all bacteria and fungi to survive the onslaught of such food and, indeed, some of us lived in spite of being exposed to such obnoxious fare. We needed food! But we, the displaced refugees caught up in active battle zones, were nobodies. We did not count, we did not exist.

The ordinary Russian soldier was equally contemptible cannon fodder, together with their comrades from the Far East and the Poles. What we had in common was hunger and the desperate desire to live. My mother saw this clearly. How to use it to the advantage of both camps? Get the soldiers to get food for all of us. Their superiors would probably not mind because it would keep their soldiers in food without putting a strain on army supplies. The soldiers were in a position to requisition (shoot) the odd animal as they were driven past us. They were few and far between as most had by now gone east and the remaining ones had collapsed from hunger and thirst. It was forbidden to requisition animals destined for Russia. But with a weapon in your hands you actually win most arguments. It was our job to go scouting for animals when they were still well away from command centres, inform friendly soldiers, they did the work and returned to their unit before anyone knew they had absconded. We would cut up the carcass, let it disappear and when cooked let the soldiers know. They turned up, officially to have their clothes washed. Their clothes were held together by dirt. The soldiers themselves were treated like dirt, and ruled with an iron fist.

I have witnessed many beatings carried out by officers and many fearful whippings using those dreaded Cossack whips. We and the ordinary soldiers led a cautious and precarious co-existence. Apart from the dirt, we ourselves were also plagued by lice and fleas, just like them. Fleas and lice are not choosy. My mother was possibly thinking of her brothers and my poor Daddy. She used to sigh, '*Die armen Jungchens*'. The poor little boys. We have to do something about this. She started washing parties. There was no soap and no washing powder, but the clothes would be boiled and did come out of the cauldron looking a beautiful dirty grey, a colour we liked so much. While your clothes were in the boil you were starkers, no one had a second set of clothing. So, some women with more than one pair of knickers would lend the spare to the soldiers, there was much laughter and at the end of the day everyone was able to walk away with clean clothing, not necessarily with the outfit they had started off with. The waiting time was passed with eating the stolen cow.

There was no longer a division between a hostile army and us, women and children. What united us was the merciless struggle for survival. No one felt like a nation apart, Polish, German, Russian, or wherever you came from, we were just people, with children snuggling up to foreign mothers and any mother of any nationality looking after some poor little child that had no one left to care for it. Language difficulties were replaced with hugs and kisses. We did get on well together. Why was there a war? Why did we fight each other? Mad!

BURYING THE DEAD

It must have been early April. The ground had begun to thaw and what happened next was really inevitable. Someone had to bury the mountains of dead. Their bodies had been lying along the roads from January onwards and as days and weeks went by, more and more were added. Their numbers were like something out of a poor horror film in very bad taste, well over the top to impress the viewers. But this was real and somehow you had to get your mind round it without going crazy. Who was to bury them? The age-old system with its reliable track record was used. 'You, you and you …' And that is how I ended up on a lorry together with lots of other children – most even younger than me – and a few really old and feeble men. Our destination was the road between Rhenitz and Soldin. I was destined not to escape this road. From the day I first walked it on 14 February I had always felt like I was being strangled so tight I could barely breathe and instead of a heart I seemed to have a heavy stone. In my imagination I still saw the long lines of people stumbling forwards in ice and snow with expressions of terror on their faces. Everyone and everything on this path to death for so many seemed haunted. Instead of the rumble of tanks and the terrifying sound of attacking aircraft there was now an eerie silence. Sounds were so far away, unreal, muffled, like being underwater. I barely perceived the rattle of lorries on the point of falling to bits, the commands of Russian soldiers heavily armed acting as our guards. One did not have to know Russian to understand what they were shouting at us. 'Get off that lorry, come over here, pick up your spade, start digging.' We just nodded. We saw what was required of us. You wanted to go to the toilet? Certainly not. That was not on the programme. No provision had been made for such irrelevant things. Wet yourself if you want to, or don't, if you don't want to.

Needless to say, we were not given any protective clothing or any suitable for the weather conditions, no gloves, no masks. Dealing with rotten bodies is not an easy matter. The condition of the decaying corpses is such that you do not touch. You dig a hole or a depression in the ground close to the body and then, using your spade, you fearfully scrape or lever it into the hollow you have made, then hastily cover it and move on to the next. There were, of course, no news crews around to take pictures of us and beam them around the world. In any case, they would have been censored as too insensitive and offensive. And yet, I have learned since then that there were many people about who would have happily watched us slaving away among the bodies. They were Germans, that served them right.

I was desperately aware of our part – my part in particular – that we were forced to play in this macabre scenario. I began to act as if I was in a surreal play. I started to talk to the bodies, frozen, dissolved by frost and thaw or shrivelled due to dehydration after death to no more than skin and bone in the clothing they wore. Sometimes there was just a smashed skull with some bones under some rotting garment. I told them that I knew they were once alive, that they had mothers and fathers and perhaps children and that they had loved them, and that they had been loved and that I was here on the behalf of their families to tell them they were loved; that

I was doing my very best to show them respect and bury them with as much dignity as I was capable of. I wished them peace and begged them to sleep, please, sleep. I offered them my humble thoughts in forms of poems. For everybody I buried I said a poem. I was aware of the shame brought upon the human race by what had happened to them.

I did not just say poems for the ones I buried myself but also for the ones I saw buried by others around me. Some children were crying. The old men were crying, they were crying for us, the children. Others like me worked on stoically. I did not cry. I continued reciting poems, then passages from works by Goethe, then extracts from the book my teacher had given me, poems my mother had taught me, then what I had learned from my grandfather, my great-grandfather. My head eventually ran out of ideas. I felt stupid. I started again. I almost panicked. It got worse. There were so many bodies that I had to allocate this poem for the group over there, that poem for the ones behind that bush, another for those in the ditch, and so on.

Then I took to singing to the bodies. I knew so many songs; would I know enough? I included nursery rhymes, anything I knew right through to *Es leuchten die Sterne*, (The Stars Shine), being my father's favourite. In short, I acted mad, perhaps I was quite mad, but it kept me sane. I was not surprised when I met up again with the 400 or so German POWs I had seen marching towards Soldin not so long ago. They had all been shot before they had reached Soldin. Mere children themselves.

It was a long job, my group worked for two days in that area. The 400 were not the only ones that needed burying. When it was done, I sang them Heinrich Heine's *Ich Weiß nicht, was soll es bedeuten* ('I know not if there is a reason'). I cannot look at the Rhein without thinking of them. Their mothers will never know what happened to them. I know. I did my best with the utmost respect and genuine grief.

I don't remember being given any food by the soldiers. Some old men had some dried food on them, which they gave to us children. They no longer had a chance of survival, so with their scraps they gave us a chance to live. A slim chance. Some children died. The worst agony was not having water. If only one could have had some water. The nights were spent under an open-sided, barn-like building. It was cold. It was torture. After three days we were told to go. Go home; wherever that was. I knew my way about in this area and found my way back to my frantic mother. The women knew roughly where we had been, while some were looking after their children, others had gone out to search for us and had reported back having seen children working away on that infamous road. So, by 1945 standards, all had ended well and I had survived another living nightmare.

Some of those nightmares I am reluctant to describe but perhaps I should for the sake of truth. Here are two.

While in the area of Rhenitz, give or take 10km, we had found shelter for just a few days on a farm with a few Russian and Polish mothers with their surviving children. I was, as usual, everybody's dogsbody. Go here, run there, fetch this, carry that, I was small, tough and fast. How I understood the many requests made to me in I don't know what language is a mystery to me today. But I observed and anticipated what needed doing and always looked very intensely at the person's face speaking to me. Fetch firewood. I did.

The women, three of them, Polish, were looking after a young German man. He had been severely beaten. He was very ill and had what I now know is a club foot. As I returned to the room with my sticks of wood to keep a fire going, four Russian soldiers burst in. They immediately made for the sick young man. They were going to show us how they dealt with a German 'soldier'. The three women tried to defend him, he had clearly never been in any army. They begged the soldiers to leave him alone and even tried physically to drag them away from their unfortunate victim. It was no use, the soldiers started beating them up as well. I tried to leave the room, but the soldiers pulled me back. A sharp click from one of their firearms made our situation crystal clear. One more move or sound and we would be shot. The women were silenced. Then one of them took me into her arms, pushed my head under her cardigan and held me there, tight. It was dark, I could barely breathe, I felt her trembling body, her heart beat faster than mine. I could not see but I could hear the young man beaten to death. It seemed to take forever before his screams and crying stopped. And that poor woman! She could not help that young man any more, but while she was trembling with compassion and fear herself, she could still protect a child. And I was not even hers. I have never come to terms with the dark.

I had mentioned before how sorry I was for mothers with very young children, they will cry at the wrong time and give the hiding place of their mothers away. One day shouting came from an outbuilding and I observed from my hideout how a Russian soldier tried to drag a young woman into the barn. She struggled clinging tightly to her little toddler. Enraged, the soldier wrenched the child out of her arms, flung it to the ground, jumped on it, stamped on it and with a final outburst of swearwords he kicked the dying little child onto a nearby dung heap.

I am a peaceful person and will always line up behind: do not kill! But I regret that I had no weapon on me when I witnessed this mindless, evil murder. How come, whenever you encounter this kind of evil, you have no weapon on you?

THE SCENT OF LILAC

Some time in early May (no one knew a date any more), early cherries opened up their blossoms and the rumour went round that the war was over. No one took any notice of these rumours. Perhaps it was, perhaps it was not. The Russian soldiers equally seemed clueless. They shook their heads and shrugged their shoulders. We were not part of the rest of the world. For us the chaos, the lack of food, the daily brutal killings of innocents by vicious men who, when left to their own devices, were out of control, did not stop. At that time I came closest to death. The circumstances were so frightening that I lost a coherent picture of how it happened.

It was in a field with hedgerows, there were people, we may have been out foraging, usually looking for remnants of potato clamps. Then I remember shouting, shooting, screaming and then silence. The silence seemed to be so loud that it hurt my head, so I got up. It was a struggle, people were lying on top of me. When I was eventually standing I looked round and saw people lying all around me.

Then I realised, of course, that we were all dead and I was the first to have woken up to find myself in heaven. They would all wake up gradually now and there would be sweet music and we would all be welcomed in heaven. And yet, it was all such an anticlimax, so disappointing. Heaven looked like the field and the bushes I vaguely remembered. I felt so lost and so lonely, not at all like light and golden sun and warmth. I almost cried as I looked round in vain for an angel. Surely, an angel would come now and show me where to go. I could not see a Golden Gate, nor St Peter to open it for me. My fear intensified. I felt paralysed, as if I was dying, which was not possible because I was dead.

Then suddenly, there was movement in the air, leaves were rustling in glittering sunshine and warm air enveloped me with an almost overpowering scent of lilac. At that moment I realised I was not dead. I had been in a massacre with bodies falling on top of me and thus shielding me from bullets. I let out a loud scream, but immediately caution told me to shut up. Where were the perpetrators of the massacre, were they still nearby? There were some things that helped me to survive. Don't touch, don't go near, shut up, melt away quietly and above all, be lucky. 'Being dead' had a lasting effect on me. For years I shivered with fear at lilac time. The scent reminded me of such a terrible past: such terror, such cold, such hunger, so much cruelty, exhaustion, deprivation, the loss of virtually everything I loved, not just highly valued personal possessions, my home, my security, my hopes for the future. I had also lost my friends, my dearest relatives and my dear little pets, my plants, my toys, my trees. I felt close to losing my sanity.

So one day, decades later, I decided to do something about these menacing memories. I had by then a home with a large back garden. I bought a lilac bush. 'Madame Lemoine'. I planted it right in view of the kitchen window. I could not miss it, looking out. It flowered the first year and looked divine. I felt very brave, I walked out of the door, along the garden path up to the lilac and without hesitation – I did not dare to hesitate – bent over the luscious blooms and breathed in the enchanting scent. I controlled my rising panic. I felt

1. Luise's mother. She fought for her children like a tiger for her cubs, with cunning and even sometimes brute strength.

2. Luise Urban, about four years old.

3. Luise Urban, pictured almost at the moment when her world began to fall apart.

4. The school that Luise first attended in 1939.

5. Germany invades Poland, 1 September 1939.

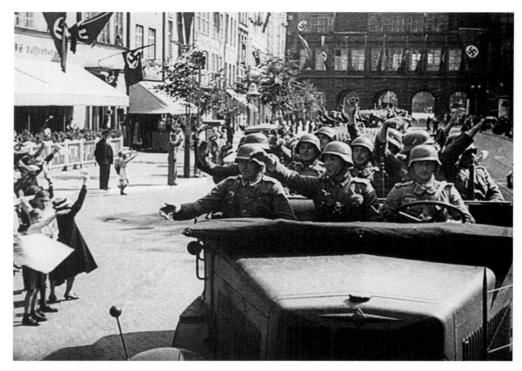

6. The German troops are greeted by cheering crowds in Danzig.

7. SA troops put up anti-semitic posters.

8. Police harassment of the Jewish community begins.

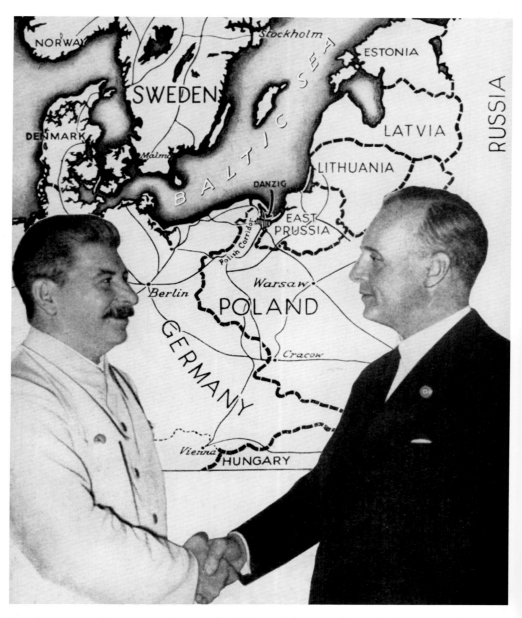

9. 23 August 1939; the agreement between the Soviets and the Nazis that made the invasion of Poland possible. Stalin and Ribbentrop shake hands in Moscow. The map in the background shows the Polish Corridor and the Free City of Danzig.

10. A Polish armoured train bombed off the track. The explosive power is indicated by the huge crater.

11. Luise's father fashioned this tin cup. He reckoned it saved his life; and at the age of 37, it was his only material possession.

12. Luise's 'Uncle Max', the boxer Max Schmeling as a paratrooper.

13. Luise's grandfather's copy of Goethe that Luise managed to keep throughout the war and still has today.

14. The factory managed by Luise's uncle.

RUDOLF ARNDT
DEXTRINFABRIK NEUDAMM
GEGRÜNDET 1884

hat sich aus kleinen Anfängen zu der ältesten und größten deutschen Spezialfabrik für

Dextrin, lösliche Stärke, British Gum
entwickelt

15. A *Volkssturmbataillon* on the Oder. Old men and young boys were instructed to fight to the death.

16. A new home in Stuttgart. The family lived in the white building to left in the far distance.

17. Collecting clothing for the *Volkssturm*.

18. Russian troops at the Oder look towards Berlin.

19. An astonishingly beautiful picture of troops at the Oder.

20. Are these civilians or soldiers left to rot? Luise was pressganged into burying the dead when the thaw came.

21. The 'monster' that Luise is sure she saw in the moonlight at the village of Zorndorf, an apparition that told her the war was lost; the ISII Joseph Stalin tank.

22. The same lesson; Russian peasants mourn for a loved one killed by the Germans.

23. Aftermath of the Dresden firestorm.

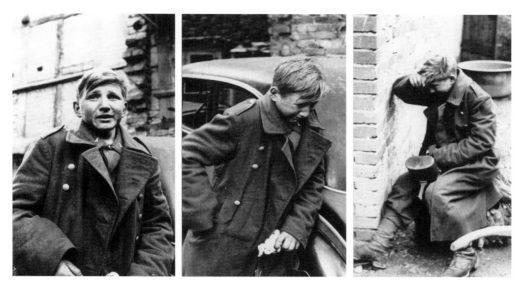

24. An unforgettable image of a Hitler Youth captured by the Americans. As Luise's mother said (and nearly died for saying it), 'All children like sweets.'

25. Kathy, Luise's daughter-in-law, Luise, her mother and Eve's brother Dietrich, September 1989.

26. Luise's ambitions to become a dancer were thwarted by the years of malnutrition she suffered as a child.

the dead deserved composure and respect. In my mind I embraced them all. I said no poems this time. Silent remembrance seemed more suited. I have looked forward to lilac time every year since then. I cannot undo the apocalypse, I can but honour the dead.

Back in spring 1945 you could not imagine in your wildest dreams that amid the despair, death and destruction, tender loving emotions and feelings could possibly flourish. At some stage, in the area of Rhenitz, where we were, a senior Russian officer was stationed. He was well above average height and well proportioned, with pleasing facial features, confidence-inspiring and with warm brown eyes, about in his early thirties. He was clearly a decisive character when among the soldiers and was obviously not promoted to officer because of his looks. He was often out and about everywhere among German refugees; he visited standing houses occupied by all kinds of refugees, usually accompanied by a translator, as he spoke no German. Here was a man who cared. We felt safe in his presence.

He could not, of course, control the hordes of Russian ruffians and prevent their offences against the civilian population, but the fact that he was about kept a lid on their violence. After only a short time he came daily to the place where we were and one day he brought a translator because he said he wanted to converse with my mother. My mother herself was glad to have someone to talk to. Vassili, that was his name, came across as highly intelligent, cultured, well read and could follow my mother on any topic. My mother matched him.

In short, the two of them developed a friendship while philosophising about God and the world and the war. Vassili connected well with children and when he turned up everyone, including me, made for him to sit on his knee. His home was in Siberia, he talked about his apparently very large property, a farm, and we knew he talked sense. He also talked about people there in general, about his family in particular. He was not married. He talked about characters in his community, about the weather, about how bad the German winters were; -20°C to -30°C or so was clearly not cold, but there was too much moisture in the air, he complained. Where he lived it was truly very cold but dry and easier to tolerate; if you threw a bucket of water in the air it would fall down as ice.

He laughed a lot and we all adored him. He wanted to help us, anyone could clearly see that we were on our last legs, particularly my little sister, she was fading away and it was truly amazing that she was still clinging to life. There was so little food. Vassili did all he could to procure something for us, including his rations. Officers were better off than the common soldier. Vassili even brought along tubes of cheese. Magic. Quite unheard of. How did I know it was cheese before the tube was even opened? It had writing on it. But I could not read Russian. So, how did I know? While Hitler was in power he had decreed that all Germans had to learn English and French from an early age. That is why I could understand what was inside the Russian army's food supply packages. The Russian army's food was largely supplied by the Americans.

He got around a fair bit and if he found something usable – a pair of trousers, a remnant of a blanket – he would bring it along for us. Not only for us, he did not forget our fellow sufferers. What he could bring was very limited. There was little to be had and Vassili did not steal. He was one of those human beings who do not have it in them to do harm to others. The war lay heavily on his conscience. Nowadays, Vassili would have been considered an aid worker.

My mother told him that he could not expect any favours from her in exchange for food for the children, as she was another man's wife. Vassili was a gentleman and said that he respected her too much for a trade. I know that because I was there when the conversation took place and I remember the translator getting a bit nervous. She told him about her grief and her fears for my Daddy. Vassili listened quietly, he said he was very saddened for us because no more had been heard since El Alamein. And one would have to face the fact that there would be little hope of him still being alive. He knew more about El Alamein than we did.

One day he came along particularly spic and span and declared through the translator that he was more than just fond of my mother, that he loved her and he wanted to marry her and look after us four children as if we were his own. He was well propertied and able to care for us all. He had enquired about all formalities, there were no objections because we were German, Russia had lost millions of people and the Russian government was taking anyone young and able to work for Russia in the future. We were all touched by the enormity of this proposal, his generous heart, his good will and honesty. I was close to tears. I knew that my mother would say no, she already had a husband. Oh, we all hurt. Vassili was very dignified, he would wait and in the meantime care for us as best as he could.

Then rumour had it that we would all have to leave and go west of the Oder. We dismissed it as idiotic because we were at home this side of the Oder, our properties and homes were here and not somewhere in another part of the world. Vassili explained that as far as he had heard, the whole area east of the Oder was to be handed over to Poland. So alright, but that was no reason to leave, what nonsense. Shall we concentrate on finding food? That was important. Then a woman who was our 'walking newspaper' announced that she definitely knew our home town had been cleared of all Germans. They had been ordered to go to the west of the Oder. We were thunderstruck. My mother gasped, 'Where is my mother?' I, my brothers and sister were assigned to a Polish mother while my mother more or less ran off to our town to see for herself what might have happened. She found no one. But in the cellar, behind a brick where we hid messages, she found a note to say that my grandmother had left two days before, together with two other old people known to her. We learned almost a year later that she was already alone by the time my mother reached our house. The three old people had come across a dead horse. The old man had said he was sure it was still edible and cooked some of it. He and his wife ate the meat. My grandmother did not. With a bit of luck it takes longer to die of starvation than poisoning yourself with dead meat. Her companions died in a day and so she struggled on alone, long before she reached Küstrin. She was found by other refugees sitting on a stone, with her mind gone, in the area of Eberswalde. Good people took her with them and left her with another kind family in that town. It took almost a year before she could even remember her name. After that the Red Cross united us again.

Back to my mother in the cellar. She left details of our whereabouts and what had happened to those relatives that had died and where they were buried. We had by now three dear relatives missing, presumed dead, or possibly POWs somewhere; and then there was grandfather, last seen alive on 31 January in Küstrin. They might come back to our house and they knew about the cellar. On her way back she looked in on a neighbouring farm and found there the very old mother of that family, confused and poorly. On the table stood a pot with boiled potatoes, which was all her family could do for her, too weak themselves to carry an invalid, they had left their mother behind. And my mother could not do anything for her either.

The mental stress for millions of us was, and still is, indescribable. Many preferred death to the continued suffering or just took leave of their senses. For some mothers, one option taken was to kill their children, the ones still alive, and then kill themselves. Let them sleep in peace. In later years I heard repeatedly some people say that it is wrong to take your own life. God sends you no more than you can bear. It shows to me that there is no God; such a wise, superior being would not create such blinkered, stupid, heartless creatures. I was, and I still am, taken aback by the large numbers of people who have no grasp of the consequences of intolerance and war. I was too hurt to argue with them and open up old wounds. My desire was to run away from crippling memories. I have so far never been able to outrun them.

THE ORDER TO GO WEST

My mother arrived back after an 80-kilometre walk late in the day, just in time for some Polish officials to order us to be gone by daybreak. 'Go west of the Oder.' Why? What had we done? We had no food, no adequate clothing, nothing to drink. Water did not come out of a tap in those days and all water supplies were contaminated. Many were too ill to be moved, many unfit to walk any distance. How can we cope and survive out in the open? Please, someone, help! No one helped. And that is how a major crime of the Second World War was committed, first discussed and planned by Winston Churchill and Joseph Stalin in 1943. They were the original partners in crime. I will have more to say on this later on.

My mother's assessment of the situation was short. We have to leave, we have one night, we have no food. Now what? We had found some fodder beets the day before. Raw they were too heavy to carry. Eaten raw they were not very nutritious either. The fodder beets were useless to us as they were. My mother ordered large

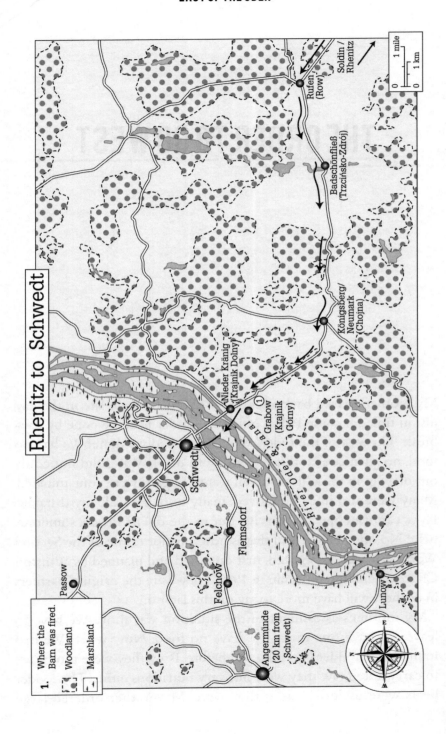

quantities to be washed, cut into small pieces, squashed, the juice to be collected and then boiled to evaporate as much water as possible in the time available to us. I felt so sorry for her. How exhausted she must have been. Walk 80km, suffer the trauma of losing your mother, walk back to us, be told to be gone by daybreak, four weak children, no sleep, no food. She worked like a zombie.

I worked in despair trying to get my jobs done as instructed. We washed, we chipped, we pressed, we boiled and in the morning had about 15 litres of black sticky liquid, so bitter it would make you sick if you took more than a couple of big spoonfuls of it. But it contained sugar. You just had to keep it down. We poured the liquid into one of the smaller milk churns which we had found, lucky us, then loaded it on to a hand cart together with my little sister and two brothers. We had nothing else to take, only the rags we wore. We were ushered out of the house at gunpoint by heavily armed Poles. My mother pulling, me pushing the cart. I was allowed my Goethe and *Don Quichote*. Vassili's unit had been relocated too far away for us to leave a message, which grieved us very much. We knew he would be devastated.

As we approached the main road leading away from the village we met up with other small groups and were straightaway confronted with more heartbreak. Among us were, of course, Polish, Russian, White Russian, Ukrainian mothers and some of other nationalities with their children. But the Polish soldiers sorted us out. Only Germans were allowed to leave. There was much crying and begging. It did not help. The Polish mother who had looked after us was smart. She put her little boy on our cart and suddenly did not understand Polish; we dragged her among our midst and in the general confusion and chaos she passed as German and she got away with us. I looked back when we had gone a few hundred metres and I will never forget all those suffering, kind women and mothers standing there in a close group in their black clothes and long skirts. Some had covered their heads with their aprons, still crying and being harassed by the soldiers. They had been our ersatz mummies in need. They had to face the new order of the world in a country that was not their home. I dread to think how many perished.

My mother thought it was best not to go back to Küstrin but that it would be better to go via Königsberg to Schwedt and cross the Oder there. Then we were back on the road again, no cover at night, no shelter anywhere, exhausted, hungry, weak. All we had to eat were a few spoonfuls of the black, bitter syrup several times a day. Nowhere to stop and boil water, nothing to drink. I remember my mother most carefully counting out the spoonfuls because the bitter syrup was all that stood between us and starvation. I also suddenly remembered my father saying to her on the last occasion when he said farewell at the end of his leave, 'Always make sure that you get enough to carry on, without you the children will be lost.' My mother had promised to look after herself. She lived her life on a knife edge.

The view from the road to the right and the left was what we had been accustomed to. Devastation, scorched earth policy, burnt buildings, no sign of any life, human or animal. Only other decrepit humans like us making slow progress in the direction of the great river. After a couple of days the weaker ones fell by the wayside. Mothers sitting by the roadside cuddling their dying children, old women still alive, sitting by the bodies of their loved ones, physically and mentally no longer able to move on. As we approached Königsberg there were noticeably fewer of us left. We dragged ourselves on past the dead lying on either side of the road littered with their pitiful belongings. My mother said, 'Don't touch the bodies.' As if I would. But we looked inside one bundle that had clearly not yet been opened by anyone. We struck lucky. The bundle contained one alarm clock and a pillow case with several pounds of sugar. I had really hoped for shoes, mine had begun to hurt and fall to pieces. To some degree we were now saved, we had bitter syrup, sugar, a pot, gas lighter fire stones, but no water. Not to have water becomes a torture.

We struggled on in the hope that in Königsberg there would be some water. There wasn't. The entire town was in ruins. The 'road' through the town had been created by all the tanks that had rumbled through it, leaving a clearance between totally destroyed, burnt-out buildings. I was not in charge of our tiny family, but my mind was racing. I felt almost as responsible for us as my mother and nodded vigorously when she said, 'We must move on, there will be water, when we are out of here.' Yes, of course, there would be, you had to believe it. The alternative was to lie down and wait to die. Rather not.

The next day we passed a farm and being familiar with farm buildings my mother and I had a quick look round. Inside an animal house we found an old-fashioned water pump. It worked. We boiled water and drank what we could, but could take none with us for lack of a suitable container. Well, we would have to move on and hope to find water ahead. We were getting closer to Schwedt. It was getting dark one day – some trees were flowering, it was that time of year, I cannot put a date to it – when we approached a barn; not normally an amazing sight, but in 1945, a barn still standing?

There was the need for shelter, rest and sleep. And yet, an undamaged barn? Unease. We walked inside, quite a few people were already in there among the straw. We stopped. My mother counted out the spoons of bitter syrup, three per person, but five for me. I knew why. I was the workhorse and needed extra rations. More people arrived, there must have been about 70 or so. My sister and brothers drifted in and out of sleep. A few more people arrived as it got dark. My mother sat up and whispered, 'I don't like it. Quickly, let us go outside and hide our cart.' We did. We returned very fast. My heart was thumping because my mother was so keyed up. Then we heard in the distance the sound of approaching army vehicles, they could only be Russian. 'Take little sis. Quick.' My mother grabbed the sleepy boys. 'Keep quiet, not a sound, follow me.' We knew the procedure. Danger. Don't be heard. Don't be seen.

We rushed past the dozing, exhausted people and through the door saw in the lorries' headlights what may have been chicken outhouses partially collapsed, with a juicy dung heap in front. My mother threw the little boys into this shed onto the dung. I dashed after them with my dainty little sister, my mother threw herself in and held tightly onto what passed as a door. Keep quiet, mousy quiet. We did. Then men's voices, shouting, screaming in the barn, shooting and then flames shot up. The screams subsided, the lorries pulled away. In spite of the increasing heat we were shivering with fear. Morning came, silence, not a soul in sight, we emerged soaked in manure, stinking to high heaven. We were alive. No one else was. Burning flesh and sparkling cinder was all that was left of the barn and our companions. Once again, my mother's nose for danger had saved us from a terrible death. I had lost my *Don Quichote*. The real blow was the loss of our aluminium pot and fire-making equipment. No fire, no water.

We made our way towards the Oder the hard way, avoiding roads, through woodland and difficult ground cover and moving silently, like Indians in North America. I had once read *The Last of the Mohicans* and made the connection. When we got near the river we found hundreds of other people there. All, like us, more dead than alive. We now became victims of Polish soldiers. They went through everyone's belongings and stole what little people had. Particularly food. All food had to be left behind. Not a scrap of a dry crust was to leave what was apparently now their country. These are the ways of the world, defenceless women and children make the best and most productive victims. There was a lot of despair and crying. The soldiers jeered and laughed.

I could not help noticing that there were a lot of mothers carrying the bodies of their children. They would not be parted from them. I felt imprisoned in my helplessness. We were by now close to the river's edge. There was a largish vessel to take us across the water. The gigantic bridge was down. I noticed a huge number of Russian tanks in the water, forming a kind of bridge. There were so many of them that one could actually get across the river with a hop and a skip, possibly without getting a foot wet. The word 'punishment battalion' sprang to mind. The tops of the tanks were closed, no damage in evidence.

A Polish soldier got a bit fresh with me. My mother watched with concern, guarding her three other children. I shouted, 'Don't worry, I can handle this.' I was speaking from experience. I won, but this little bastard of a man took one of my shoes off and threw it in the river.

The river was deep, dangerous and fast flowing with a concrete embankment. I should have been glad he had not pushed me in. It would have been my death. But I was so furious I took my other shoe off and threw it in as well. The soldier became even more furious than me. That's when my mother stepped in. She was livid. She apologised to the soldier for my rude behaviour, clipped my ears several times and hissed, 'Will you never learn?' The soldier enjoyed the spectacle and I saw my mother's point of view. You do not antagonise an already hostile moron of a soldier. If he takes your shoe and throws it into the river then the message is, your shoes are his shoes, he clearly told you so by his actions and if he chooses to throw one of your shoes into the river, then it does not mean that you have the right to throw the other in as well. What is yours and what is not yours is decided by a stupid brute and you have no say over it. It was pathetic. But there I was, a slow learner.

When the scuffle was over, my mother approached another Polish soldier. Could he get us to the front of the queue in exchange for an alarm clock? He could. My mother always picked the right person. We found ourselves on the other side of the river perhaps less than two hours later and out of Polish jurisdiction. We were in no-man's-land, in a water desert. The Oder is not the kind of river you may have in mind when you only know the rivers in Great Britain. The Oder is a giant of a river carved by the Ice Age, with two arms and one canal in the area of Schwedt. Full and fast flowing in spring with bridges down and embankments burst, we were faced with a mass of swirling, deep water full of bloated corpses of animals and humans. The waters of the river in this area were at least three kilometres wide, interspersed with patches of drifting sand forming low muddy islands with their edges continually being washed away. We gazed at the sight in fear.

There were perhaps four or five German men about. How had they got there? Who knows? Who cares? They had two boats, little boats, they rowed us across to the next largish island. Only two or three persons at a time. The boats were not large enough to take more and each boat already had a rower in it. The men took turns rowing back and forth, they had no strength and the river was wild. Here and there someone had got away with a scrap of food and gave it to the men as a thank you for rowing them across. Most of the food had of course been taken away by the Poles. When we landed on the last island, there was no boat. But there was a tree and there were more trees on the other side of the water. There were only three men, a rope tied to the tree, the other end of the rope attached to one of the trees at the far side of the water. Most of the rope was invisible in the water; and then there was the transport itself. A table top attached ingeniously to one of the men who hauled himself, the table top and what could be loaded on it along a guide rope across the water. That was truly scary. The table top was underwater and only one large person or two children could be taken across at a time.

There was a young mother with a bundle containing a small child's body in her arms and clinging on to another skeleton of a child. She asked the men to take her across. All she had left were her last two children, one dead, one still alive. 'I have buried one already,' she said. The men considered taking the dead child but not for long. They said 'No. For everybody we take across, a living child has to stay behind. More are arriving, many will have to stay on this mud patch overnight.' The poor mother was perfectly composed. 'Yes,' she said, 'I understand, take me across with my little one and, please, bury my baby for me.' The men nodded. Of course, tomorrow they would take the dead baby across and bury it over there, they pointed at a particular tree on the far side. She was hauled across with her last child. We, who had heard this conversation, found the decision sensible: the living had to come first. And hadn't we all buried someone else's nearest and dearest? I thought, yes, lots and lots of them.

Then it was my turn to be ferried across. I was tied to the man who operated the rope by the other man who stayed behind on the island, while the third man waited on the other side to untie people and to unload the goods. In this case the milk churn, which I had to hang on to. Because of its weight it went across untied because if it sank it would perhaps take the table top with it. That was too much of a risk. Then our hand cart, on its own. It was made of wood and would float, but it took up too much space on the table top for anyone else to cross at the same time. Then my sister and big brother, then my mother and my little brother. All duly tied together and attached to the man with the rope. He was clearly handicapped by the people roped to him and it was very hard work. The mass of water was flowing fast. No surprise then that they would not take a body when there were so many living children still to be saved. How they managed to go on doing this rescue work I don't know, their feet were permanently in ice-cold water. But they were calm and spoke kindly to us children, who had to go across without our mummies and were frightened out of our wits. I was actually a very good swimmer but if something had gone wrong, I realised that no one would have been able to survive in that current.

I assembled the cart while the others were ferried over. Then all of us had to make it up a steep, sandy embankment with the river valley below us. It was such hard work, my brothers and sister had no strength even to crawl, the cart had wheels but they would not move in the sticky sand, the incline was too steep and my mother struggled with the milk churn. After an eternity we all stood on top of the valley at the point of collapse. I was at the end of my tether and gasped: 'Water, water, a kingdom for some water.' Please, don't tell me I am making this up. I am not. I know what I said was based on *Richard III*; thanks to my grandfather I was as familiar with Shakespeare as I was with Goethe. We turned towards the cart ready to load the children and move on when my mother said, 'Stop a moment, turn round and look at the land beyond the Oder ... *Das ist eure Heimat* ... That is your homeland.' An unforgettable sight. Silver Sand, *Märkischer Sand, dunkle Kiefernwälder*, dark pine forests. *Meine Heimat*. I have never seen it since.

Why am I no longer there? In time-honoured fashion, the victors after a war divided the land among themselves, to appease or reward allies. One lot would give another lot a chunk of land as a gift or traded it in for something else in return. My *Heimatland* was given to Poland. Not something like the size of, let us say, Wales, no, larger than Ireland, larger than Scotland, more than three times the size of Holland and Belgium put together. Similar nonsense was concocted after the First World War and before that and before that, ad infinitum.

Before 1945, the people in these requisitioned lands were made over to the victors as well. Can you think of anything more idiotic? As the population in Europe and the rest of the world increased, more and more people living in these areas became affected. In the 20th century millions suddenly found that they were now French, or Polish, or German, or Russian. My close relatives who once ran away from their land and heritage because they did not want to be Polish and the persecution this entailed for them were just one example of the consequences of such crude, cruel and mindless policies.

In effect, the First World War, at least for Germany, never stopped. The hardships after that war for the population were insufferable; people were looking for a way out by hook or by crook, and the seething unrest around the new borders did not allow the country to rest. I remember that my family in 1919 took out a huge mortgage secured on the property, just to survive. Some attic rooms were full of suitcases with money. My grandmother explained that it would take a whole wheelbarrow-full of money to buy one loaf.

Together with the prospect of having to pay for ill-thought-out reparations at a level which would in all likelihood result in non-cooperation, even rebellion, was disillusion and depression. Depression mentally and economically. Small wonder agitators and nationalists emerged. You may say I see the world in a simple way. And I do. The population of the world around the turn of the century had become huge, numbers that no government at that time could deal with. And who was in charge? Mainly hereditary monarchies. And who was at the head of some very big important nations in Europe? Idiots. Kaiser Wilhelm, Nikolaus II and King George V, the latter merely a figurehead behind which the state could hide. The monarchies had been in power long after their sell-by date. After the Sarajewo murder, not surprisingly, no one knew what best to do, except honourably to beat one another up. And the alliances in those years were such that if one was in for a beating, all were in for it. Common sense had gone out of the window. The one that comes off worst is then declared the loser and also the one whose fault it was and therefore has to pay compensation and eat humble pie. In spite of the disastrous outcome – the Second World War – there was no one there to see the light. Hypocrisy and mind-boggling stupidity ruled. In this bitter fight for survival, terrorism and nationalism found a place at the forefront.

German newspapers declared in January 1933 with great relief that the threat of Hitler's Party had passed, that many had denounced his Party as being too extreme and that their membership was dwindling. How did it happen that he could become Chancellor at the end of the month with only a minority vote? Not only that, before long Hitler outlawed all other parties. The trap had shut. How do you get rid of a dictator? I am writing this at a time with 'elected dictatorships' in power in Iran and Zimbabwe. There were some brave attempts to remove Hitler from power. But in the end it was only Hitler who could kill Hitler. By the time Hitler was dead, millions upon millions of innocents had been dragged to their deaths. I consider myself a victim, a victim of intolerance, gutlessness and unbelievable stupidity. My unfortunate fate was avoidable and the Allied forces compounded my misfortune.

I have strayed away from the moment when I looked back at my *Heimatland* from the wrong side of the Oder. I am grateful to my mother that she made us aware of defining moments in our lives. She had called me back to have a last look at our home on 13 February 1945. 'You will never see anything like this again,' she had said. And now she had called all of us back to say, '*Das ist eure Heimat.*'

WEST OF THE ODER

We made off in the direction of Schwedt. There would be water and people who would shelter us, as we had sheltered others in the past. We and others walked on looking ahead for a glimpse of the town. I ached all over. My feet were wrapped in the sleeves cut off a jacket. You slip into the sleeve, twist it round and pull the other half back above your ankle and tie it up with string. Very bad, but better than nothing. We just could not see Schwedt: we could not be on the wrong road could we? Then we realised what had happened. The devastating truth dawned on us.

Schwedt was no more. The town had been razed to the ground; 85% had been destroyed, the remainder was no more than two or three bricks high, that is why we could not see the town. There would be no shelter, no water, nothing. There were bushes, more small canals, mud, and cold, filthy water. We were hungry, thirsty, cold, almost comatose. We sank to the ground and passed into oblivion. When morning came we found ourselves still alive. My mother

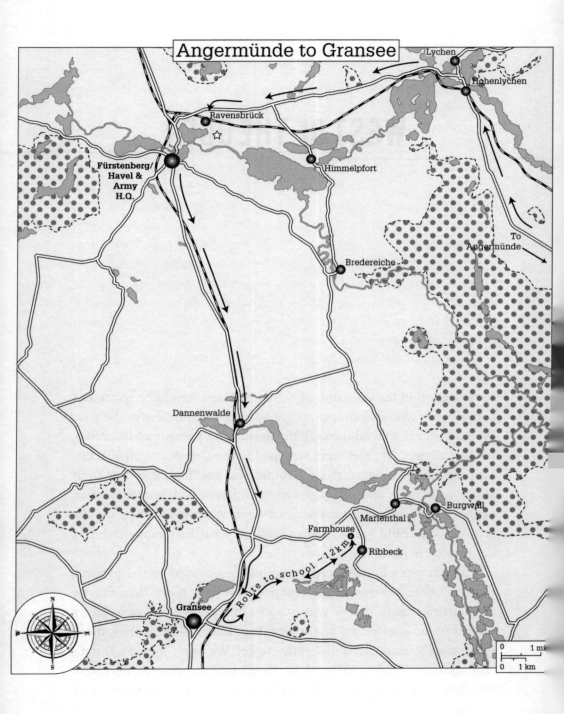

Angermünde to Gransee

Lychen
Hohenlychen
Ravensbrück
Himmelpfort
Fürstenberg/ Havel & Army H.Q.
Bredereiche
To Angermünde
Dannenwalde
Burgwall
Marienthal
Farmhouse
Ribbeck
Route to school ~12 km
Gransee

0   1 mi
0   1 km

stumbled over to an old woman nearby to ask whether by any chance she had fire and a pot. Next to her lay her husband. He had died during the night. The old woman gave my mother firestones and a pot. She would not need them any more, she intended to stay by her dead husband's side to die. By the looks of her, she would not have to wait too long.

But we boiled water, had our rations of bitter syrup and set off again. There were very few with us on the road now. 'We must go on further,' said my mother, 'there is no food here. We must get into villages again.' We didn't. The destruction was total. Instead, we arrived in Angermünde, about ten kilometres on. Some houses were standing, completely overcrowded. We crowded in as well. We may have stayed two or even three days to rest and recover and drink as much as we could. And again, my mother drove us on. 'There is no food, there will be no food, there are far too many people too close together and you know what happens then. Typhus happens.' Off we trudged again.

We found a lonely, very large farmhouse, totally deserted, no person, no animal in sight. We moved in for a rest. I found in a shed a bag with dried peas from last year's harvest, still in their shells, we shelled them, they were not mouldy and while my mother boiled them I walked about the rest of the previous owner's house. I found the library. Another highlight of my life. I took away Swedish Selma Lagerlöf's nature adventure *Niels Holgersen und seine wundersame Reise mit den Wildgänsen* and *Bibi* by the Danish Karin Michaelis. I knew they would be an extra weight to carry but my mother just nodded. 'Of course, we will take the books.' I still have the books so many decades later.

When all the peas were eaten up, which took many hours (our pot held only a small quantity and we had to have a boil-up several times), we continued our journey on the open road. It was early summer. The sun shone hot, the tar on the road melted and the heat haze obscured our vision. My little brother collapsed and vomited with heat stroke. A Russian lorry nearby had some soldiers rest-ing in its shade. My mother walked over to ask for help. Since we had made the acquaintance of Vassili, we had lost our mistrust of the Russians. And sure enough, like the majority of human beings they were friendly, they had water, they tipped water over my little brother's head, loaded us on their lorry and asked 'Where to?' Anywhere, away from the border, said my mother. They were going to somewhere near Ravensbrück. Yes, please, said my mother, thank you very much, we would be going wherever they would be going. After a lengthy drive, passed with well-meaning conversation, they unloaded us outside a farmhouse and knocked at the door with their rifles. The door was opened by a middle-aged woman, the soldiers shoved us in, they said goodbye. We had arrived, the new guests.

Living with the elderly woman was a younger one, a former POW who had stayed with the people she had been allocated to. Like our former POWs, she had lived in a camp nearby and together with others had walked back and forth to the farm every day. They had made friends and when the Russians arrived the younger woman had decided to stay with her friend on the farm. When the Russians opened the camp they found that the German guards had killed hundreds of prisoners in another part of the camp. The younger woman said that she and her nearest companions did not have the slightest idea of what had been going on at the other end of the camp. They had all been segregated and while some had walked to work on farms unsupervised, elsewhere others had been killed. Both women sobbed their eyes out and my mother rushed from the kitchen into the garden when she also broke down in tears. The murderous treachery and falsehood of the Nazi regime was exposed once more. I ran after my mother before explaining to the two women that all this had been too much for her, they should not have told her; I shouted wild things about this wicked world.

Well, we survivors had nerves of steel, or perhaps no nerves left at all to upset ourselves further, and proceeded with the business of living. I was relieved that I was not called upon to bury someone and while the women prepared some food I was sent into the garden to relax, whatever that was. In the garden was a little pond and by that pond I had a most wonderful time. It was warm, the scent of fresh grass was in the air, the sun glittered gold-green through the leaves, there was a wealth of insects, birds and tiny frogs. From the reeds emerged two of the most beautiful, elegant creatures, as much as two metres long it seemed to me, as if they had just come out of a fairy tale with crowns on their heads: grass snakes. They were not really crowns, golden half-moon markings on their heads made them look like enchanted princesses and I dared not move at the sight of such beauty. They were like a greeting from another world, they did not even know there was such a thing as war. That short afternoon was such a joy, I still remember it with great affection.

We did not stay long at this farm. My mother was too traumatised already and we perceived the closeness of the Ravensbrück camp as such a threat that all we wanted was to get away from there, we had already endured too much. One of the women had found me a pair of shoes and my feet thought they were in heaven, bare feet are not really made for long-distance walking.

During the past few months my mother and I, because of Vassili's company, had picked up enough Russian to get by in that language. A Russian unit was stationed nearby, my mother walked up to the guards and explained she had three sick children and asked could they give us a lift out of this town to somewhere in the country? An officer was called and he offered a lift to a farm near Ribbeck by the Havel, there his unit was occupying a large farm that was supplying them with food. Everyone thought my mother was mad trusting a Russian soldier; we thought, why not? Russians are people like anyone else. We pulled our cart with the three children who looked now truly at death's door to the gatehouse and shortly after we were loaded onto a lorry and taken to, amazingly, a working farm.

While most of their animals had gone, been driven away or shot for food, they still had a fair few left, including chickens, geese and 48 cows, when originally they housed over 150. The Russian army could not live on thin air, they were far too far away from Russia and there was little food left there to ship on anyway, so they did what all armies do, they lived off the land. Though in this case it was organised, not simple requisition of necessities from the locals.

The farm was full of women and children, destitute like us, and we were allocated a section of a building normally used for calf rearing. There were bundles of straw, a workbench, a small window and swallows' nests on the high ceiling. My mother got on well with the owner of the property, a resolute woman in her forties whose husband and only son had gone missing in Russia, her husband believed killed; but she did not accept it. Many could not accept the death of a close relative.

Anyway, the two women got on well, they reigned over all of us. The main job was to make sure that army supplies were met, no ifs and no buts. The Russians were our masters and must not be displeased. The soldiers collected their quota on a daily basis, punctually and all of it, leaving us very little to survive on, but that little was better than nothing. We called our surplus the leftovers and the leftovers had to feed many a hungry mouth.

I was allocated to cows together with Helen, a girl of about twelve years of age, and a decrepit old gentleman who kept losing his glasses. That left Helen and me cleaning and feeding the cows, taking them from one grazing area to another. Too much clover in this field, move the cows on to another field and another before going back home in the evening. We had to milk the cows, a very hard job for two skinny girls. We had to do it properly, otherwise their yield would collapse and the milk churns had to be filled come what may. The old gentleman looked after the bull. What a cushy number. Helen and I also had to clean the milking parlour, very hard work, and cleaning and scrubbing the churns was quite exhausting, the sheer weight of the churns was disheartening. The full churns were lifted by the soldiers onto their lorries and returned, not necessarily in the right order, with sour milk coagulated inside some of them. Helen's and my heart sank when we received those back for cleaning. If you do not clean these meticulously, the fresh milk will go sour almost instantly. By the way, we had still not been told that the war was over but we all assumed that it was.

Then my mother heard that a school had opened in a neighbouring village. It was not really a school, but a very kind-hearted retired teacher had offered to take children of all ages and teach what he could in a building that had a large room still intact. This old gentleman was there from first thing in the morning until it was getting dark. Of course, we did not have electricity. Only the fittest children went to school, about sixty of us. No particular hours were kept. School started when you arrived and you stayed as long as you could. There was a constant coming and going all day long and this very kind old teacher attended to each child personally. Some stayed for an hour or so, some for half a day and virtually all of us had very long walks to get there. In my case twelve kilometres.

I loved every minute of school. Our teacher was very fond of Goethe and Schiller and we really hit it off. I also had the advantage of sometimes being given a lift by the Russian soldiers, as they went back and forth on this route, transporting their supplies and I had an opportunity to practise my Russian. I was the only child to go to school from the village we were in, most children were too poorly to be burdened with the extra stress. They were in most cases too small to undertake a long walk and it was considered to be too dangerous for them to be anywhere but close to their mothers.

I was by then used to extreme danger and washed, as they say in German, with all waters. My mother felt she could trust me to be careful and alert at all times and at the same time not to miss an opportunity to learn something. Another young man joined the teaching staff. He was not a teacher but willing to pass on what he knew about mathematics. And a third offered help. On the blackboard he wrote '*Regina rosas amat*'. 'Now tell me something about Latin.' What a brilliant approach! We had been starved of knowledge for so long and could not get enough of all the new things.

So summer and autumn passed. Many children still died. They had survived the first half of 1945 but then faded away. It had all been too much to bear. By this time people were trying so hard to find out what had happened to lost members of their families. All families had been torn apart, there were no postal services, and if there had been, to whom were you going to write? Which town? Which address? What was left was rubble and chaos. During the war you would get your letters back, marked 'bombed out'. Now you did not even get that. In our case, it had been my father's sister in Berlin who had kept the threads of our widespread family together. Until the day when letters came back with the dreaded message. That happened to millions and made it so particularly hard to find out about each other. We, from the East, were now totally cut off and that is why my father, who had survived El Alamein and was now a POW in Oran and my mother's youngest brother, a survivor of Monte Cassino and a POW in San Francisco, were unable to locate us.

My mother had no one left to whom to turn for information. People became ill with worry and depression; that winter of 1945/46 killed many, a large number of them suicides. We had by then registered with the Red Cross, who had names and addresses of millions of people. The Red Cross was very well organised. They managed to put families together again by the million. It took time. There were no computers in those days. Thank you, Red Cross.

One day, in late 1945, the impossible happened. My mother's eldest brother, Horst, stepped into our calf shed. Silence. We recognised each other. They fell into each other's arms and wept silently. But not me, crying was an expression of emotion I was no longer capable of. It had become meaningless to me. Out of all the people, it was Horst, with the least chance of survival, who came back to us. He had been lost, presumed dead, in Russia in 1942. He had been captured, sent to a labour camp and from there allocated to a couple with a farm. They had lost their only son right at the beginning of the war. My uncle felt very much out of place to be with them instead of their son and tried his hardest to help and comfort them.

Uncle Horst was highly intelligent and picked up Russian very fast. He was also very clever with his hands and had a keen interest in physics; by trade he was an electrician who had achieved his Master's aged just 26 in Berlin. He soon became indispensable to the whole community in that Russian village. The old couple grew very fond of him, when the war was over they wanted to adopt him and officially had him declared their heir. They asked him to bring his German family over to Russia and they offered to do anything for him.

He knew his answer would be heartbreak for them, he begged them to understand his choice, which was to get home as quickly as possible to try to find his family and other relatives. Would they try to get him released? They did, and that is how it happened that out of all the prisoners taken in Russia with a next to zero chance of ever getting back home again, he was released shortly after the war ended and discharged to the western side of the Oder.

It was then he learned that the entire east of the Oder had been cleared of Germans. He was not allowed to cross the river and there he stood like many thousands of others in despair, not knowing where to turn to and how to find out what had happened to his loved ones. It took some time before our names and present whereabouts filtered through the Red Cross records and he was put in touch with us. This was such an unexpected gift. We had actually given up on him.

The Russian unit in Ravensbrück wasted no time in calling upon his services; apart from his skills he had the knack of getting on well with everyone (a bit of a diplomat). His immediate future was secure, he was accommodated in the army's officers' block. The Russians needed a lot of replacements and repairs to their communication systems and they had next to no trained people available.

The 1945/46 winter was oh so cold. We had no warm clothing. We had grown out of everything, there were no new garments, what we still had was threadbare, full of holes and held together with a piece of string, if you had one. I remember I had a warm blouse, but no jacket, no coat, but a very long, green, warm skirt. I insisted on going to school. Once I got very tired on my way there and just sat down in the snow for only a minute, but fell asleep. I was lucky again. Another person happened to walk the same way and I was saved. Of course, you never sit down in snow with inadequate clothing and go to sleep. I had not intended to snooze.

As I have said before, survival is occasionally entirely due to pure luck. That winter we had just about enough food to survive but not enough to make up for what we have not had in the previous 12 months. My brothers became very weak and began to look suntanned, strange. Much later I learned that it was due to a serious type of vitamin B complex deficiency. My little sister grew thinner and thinner, whatever food we put into her had no effect. There was the permanent cold and no heating. We were nevertheless in a privileged position, living in a building that was draught- and rain-proof. We also had more food than town dwellers.

Then one day in spring, a letter from the Red Cross arrived with the details of our grandmother, now at an address in Ludwigslust in Mecklenburg. It had taken so long to trace her because her memory had not returned for many months and she could not remember her name or where she came from. After the war, records showed that this kind of 'mental shut down' was not uncommon. It seems to be some kind of survival strategy of the brain. While able to go through the routine of looking after yourself in a mechanical sort of way you are protected from further trauma that might render you unable to cope with existing stresses and it also stops more hurt being piled onto you. It will not be me who will feel compelled to do research into this condition.

The German authorities had tried very hard to spread all those driven out of the East into areas where some form of housing was still available and where food could be distributed. And with hindsight, I fully appreciate the tremendous work that was done. It was not just houses that were destroyed, so was the transport system, all forms of communication including postal services no longer existed, such simple things as paper and pens were unavailable. There was no harvest, no food in storage, no corn, no potatoes ready for planting in spring, nothing. The most primitive requirements with which to make a start of anything of any kind were totally lacking. And what there was, was requisitioned by the Allies. It was a heartbreaking position to be in.

Then, progress apparently. Ration cards were issued. For all they were worth, you might just as well have eaten the paper, the goodies theoretically due to you were fantasy. There was *no food*. There were no rations on the cards. With hindsight it is funny that both the Nazi and the communist bureaucracies could so effectively organise paperwork but not the necessities of life. Ration cards yes, food no.

Letters were exchanged between my mother and grandmother and the decision was made that we should move to Ludwigslust, live in a real house, rent-free of course, because the homeless were allocated to house owners, just like people who had lived with us in 1944 and early 1945; no one queried this arrangement. People had to have a roof over their heads and live somewhere and soon, oh please, soon life would get better. That was the theory. It didn't work out that way.

One aspect that swayed my mother in favour of moving into a town was the chance of returning to something like a civilised environment: there would be ration cards, but above all, there would be a school. So, one day, very early in the morning we walked for many kilometres to the nearest operational railway station to wait for a train to Ludwigslust. There were no timetables, you stayed at the station until a train arrived. The Russian soldiers had clubbed together and had given us what I think was called *Alliierten* (Allies) *Mark*, apart from that we had nothing to take but our cart and my three books. The generosity of the soldiers was quite Russian, in those days violence and compassion lived cheek by jowl.

Towards the end of the day a train arrived. We had been up since about 4am already, we were hungry, we were thirsty as usual, and it was late at night. It was very dark, street lights were quite unknown to me. We found ourselves in our new town, our new abode. We asked our way to where grandmother lived, my mother and me taking it in turns to give the little ones a piggyback. They just could not walk any more and we carried them from street corner to street corner. We arrived in a very lovely street with majestic chestnut trees on either side of a very wide road with well-built, imposing houses. Not one of them damaged. Well, there are things in this world you would not believe to be true.

We found the right house number and knocked. Two very old ladies opened up, we introduced ourselves and my grandmother was called. The awfully frail, thin figure that came to the door was a shadow of her former self, heartbreaking, but it was her, it was her fine smile, so controlled and quite in charge of the situation. We were overjoyed, overwhelmed but too exhausted to waste energy on anything else but a hug and a quick, grateful kiss. By now the whole house had been woken up and some people had gone to fetch neighbours in spite of the late hour. Women arrived, children arrived, they all congratulated us; in those days it was such a moving event when a family was reunited with lost loved ones that all wanted to be there to witness and be a part of it. The women brought some feather beds, hot acorn coffee and even a cup of some vegetable soup for us. We retired to seventh heaven.

OUR NEW SOCIALIST FRIENDS

The next day my mother registered us at the town hall and Kommandantura. That was the Russian authority without whose permission nothing could be done. We were given some *Alliierten Mark* and ration cards. My mother was told that she would get extra if she declared my father dead but she did not. The other disadvantage was that she could not get any extras if she did not join the Communist Party, which she could not, because to become a Communist you had to be denazified and as we had not been in the Nazi Party we could not be denazified. There you have it. The new regime specialised in needling people. The daily calorie allowance was 800 per day for a grown-up and 400 to 600 per day for a child, according to age. No one seemed to be the right age for the 600. The problem with the allowance was that there was only vinegar and soft soap for sale. One may not be able to eat it but thanks to vinegar, soft soap and the indomitable energy of the German housewife, the country was clean, there were no major outbreaks of cholera and typhus, which you expect as routine; so you could die in peace and quiet of starvation. And thousands and thousands did just that.

To my great delight, there was school. I seemed to be a tough nut, I could apparently live on nothing, but still have lots of energy and I was an enthusiastic learner, just bring it on, I would devour it. My little sister also insisted on going to school but she was too weak to walk there, so my mother used our handcart to wheel her to school and back. This very pretty, no, very beautiful, little girl, so highly intelligent and imaginative and artistic, had very little time left in life. As she was very weak she was allocated an extra ration of skimmed milk every other day. But in a socialist country live socialist cows; and they don't give milk. They did before they became communists but their habits changed with change of ideology. My little brothers were declared unfit to go to school, they were suffering from that rare form of vitamin B deficiency. They were too ill and weak even to stand. They were no exceptions and in good company, as there were many thousands of children afflicted with the same condition. We all suffered from boils and deep, pus-filled craters on our legs, said to be caused by TB.

School was an escape and heaven on earth. Our teachers were not teachers by profession, they volunteered with some knowledge in some field and were eager to pass on to this young, long-suffering generation something they hoped would be of some use. Capitalist languages were not allowed, so English and French were out. German was out, not completely out because people did not understand much else, but reduced to two forty-minute periods per week. Russian was in. We tried hard to learn it. This was very difficult. Our teacher was the official translator from the *Kommandantura*. He arrived as a rule too drunk even to sit in his chair and his lessons were completely out of control and a free-for-all. I did my utmost to utilise his scrambled brain and thoroughly enjoyed that truly wonderfully expressive and sensitive language. Pity about the teacher.

I was fascinated by the unusual use of some verbs, eg to want – I want to learn. This 'I want' can become reflexive and the 'I' in the nominative becomes in the reflexive form the accusative. I cannot find such a construction in German, French, English or Latin. It complicated the learning of Russian but I felt drawn to it and felt that I would be able to express myself in this language. Alas, whenever I needed some advice or further explanations from our teacher I was unable to wake him up at the desk. He was always in the process of sleeping it off. By the way, later, in West Germany, I had a teacher who had majored in *Germanistik* and Russian. The trouble there was that Russian was not on the timetable. Neither Russia nor West Germany were far-sighted and organised enough to teach this important and widely spoken language when they should have.

Back to the German Democratic Republic (GDR), the Russian-occupied section of Germany. We were so restricted in our timetable that we formed secret little groups and met with our teachers outside school, somewhere in a park or walking around in the countryside. When we found a suitable, quiet corner we would sit down on the grass and learn English, French or Latin. The same applied to German literature.

Sometimes we met in someone's house, pretending we were going to a party or someone had a birthday. I even went to Bible readings (with hindsight not a wise activity under a communist regime), music lessons, gymnastics, dancing parties, any lecture on anything. I was there.

History lessons became tainted. I learned that I had lived in a shack, in great poverty. I had been slaving away for a rich capitalist dandy, but now I enjoyed the freedom of communism. Oh dear, I remembered the last look at our house, the moment when I lost my shoes and tried hard to shake off the stigma of being a slow learner. And I found it so hard to dissimulate.

Near disaster hit me in another form. There were going to be elections. All sorts of candidates for various parties had posters up wherever there was a space for it. And the SED, the Socialist Unity Party of Germany, came up with the proposal to allow youngsters from only 12 years of age to have voting rights. We were suitably enlightened about our progressive and pioneering spirit in hours and hours of talk by Party members at school. By the end of two weeks or so of bombardment with these high-flying ideologies we were asked to write an essay about the advantages of being able to vote from the age of 12 onwards. Who was stupid again? Me. I wrote that at the age of 12 one was still too close to being a child with insufficient experience in life to vote for a particular political leaning. Guess whose turn it was to be arrested this time? And again I heard my mother say, 'Will you never learn?'

I was to be questioned the next day before a committee about my knowledge of Russia and Russia's aims for the world and how to make the world a better place through communism. Well, I passed with flying colours, having lied myself black in the face. Isn't there a French saying that gently rephrases lying as being blessed with the ability to imagine when needed? I was that person so blessed and I rewrote my essay under supervision. I must have got an A with three stars because they let me go.

The elections were now coming nearer and my mother was still worried about me in case I slipped up somehow, as we expected our votes to be spied on. We need not have worried. On the eve of the election our street representative called upon us, as he did on everyone, with the good news that no one in this house needed to go out to vote, because knowing that everyone in this house would vote SED, he, our street representative, would vote on our behalf for the entire street and he would queue up on the stroke of midnight outside our community centre to cast the street's vote at 7 o'clock sharp because the street that voted first would get a star above the entrance door and he would earn this honour for us. What a hero!

My mother was, as usual, perfect when faced with something as apparently straightforward as voting for a party. There was something sinister hiding behind the simple words. Having lived under Hitler's regime she had plenty of experience in interpreting such harmless communications as the one from our street representative. It called for immediate and appropriate action. She did what she had done intuitively on 1 February 1945, when she had hugged and kissed the Russian soldiers. Now she flung her arms round the neck of our representative. Such ambition! Such inspiration for us all! At long last she was living with a regime that cared for its people. What a relief for a mother with four children not to be burdened with chores that could so easily be taken on by our comrades. She lied so convincingly that an Oscar would have been her reward nowadays without a quibble. It was vintage mother.

I have said before, my mother had a sense for danger. And that friendly, helpful man was sending out a warning to everyone: don't you dare to go anywhere near an election booth. This warning was instantly picked up by my mother. Her reaction, phony as it was, was also instantly picked up by our street representative. He, smarter than most, had figured out which direction the hare would run. Hence his job, his rations and privileges. He recognised in my mother another smart operator. Not blubbing about political tactics is important, so a reward for informed silence was in order. He returned the next day with a job recommendation for the Russian Army unit in our area. The unit was several thousand strong. The job: work in the kitchen, meaning food. He also gave us open-ended tickets for six for the People's soup kitchen. Thank you, Tovarish.

Some states use somewhat forceful methods of persuasion to attain their visionary aims. One has just been mentioned. Another popular road to success was followed by Hitler. Forbid all parties that don't agree with the illusions and delusions of the one and only leader and hold no elections at all. Pity the country and its millions of victims who are trapped in a dictatorship. There is no way out. How does one get a dictator in the first place? How do you catch a life-threatening infection? Best if you are debilitated already. A debilitated country is most likely to end up with a dictator. With hindsight, the disaster that befell Germany is a classic case. Worst of all, it was avoidable. But there were no competent, far-sighted statesmen around at that time in history, and as I have said before, the Royal Houses in Europe were not known for their intelligence.

Back to the job with the enemy's army. Sorry, slip of the tongue. I mean 'our new socialist friends'. Would you expect to get paid working for your friends? At least 12 hours per day, every day?

Certainly not. If you were offered pay for your work, you would be offended and turn it down! Under Hitler you would surely not expect to be paid working for your Fatherland. Well, people have noble feelings. I remember my grandmother being asked by the Hitler regime whether she expected to be paid working for her Fatherland when she was 'volunteered' for factory work.

The reward for working in your socialist friends' kitchen was the opportunity to steal food. Naturally, you had to be prepared to lose a percentage to the Russian soldiers who manned the check-out points on the way home. They always felt peckish and fleecing the women workers was standard. So, if you were a soldier and needed extra food for yourself or anything that might come in useful for bartering, then harass, bully, threaten and skin the mothers. Most of them always tried their hardest to get away with some food hidden in their bags for their children. With power on their side, the soldiers always lifted a lot of the precious food that these hard-pressed women managed to stash away on themselves, meant for their starving children. Much of it went down the hatch of comparatively well fed men with round cheeks.

I think of this every time when I see in newspapers or on TV pictures of unrest, strife and violence, one cannot fail to see well fed men alongside skinny women with skeletal, dying children. I feel sick at the sight of so much shameless brawn over brain. Unless you live in peaceful surroundings with law and order in place, you need a disproportionate amount of brain to overcome just a little bit of brawn. We were fortunate that my mother had the extra. That extra cunning was converted into 12 to 15 potatoes per day.

Then another joyous event. The Red Cross wrote to us concerning the whereabouts of my grandfather, whom I had last seen on that night of 31 January 1945. He was in a home for severely debilitated people, meaning close to death from starvation. Küstrin had been an area of heavy fighting, but was then bypassed by the Russian army. Why fight for Küstrin when you should be going to Berlin? Which is what they did. I believe Küstrin was not taken until after 8 May. The town was a very good fortress and virtually impossible to take since the time of Frederick the Great. But times and technology had moved on since then. I did say that the *Volkssturm* was not supplied with uniforms, there weren't any. Most importantly, they were not even supplied with a *Stahlhelm* (tin hat) either. It may be frivolous of me to ask whether they had any weapons. I know that my grandfather did not take as much as a peashooter with him. But I know that he had taken his black cap. My grandmother had lined it for him with cotton wool because he always felt so cold and already had arthritis. This cap saved his life. A bullet aimed at his head was stopped and becme entangled in the cotton wool. After a lengthy recovery, he, like uncle Horst, also walked back to the Oder trying to look for all of us. He, too, was left standing there broken-hearted and deeply grieved. When you are that old after a long life full of disappointments, hardships and deprivations, you face a mental abyss and we were so grateful that he had the strength and courage to stagger on and do everything he could to try to find us.

We choked back tears of joy and relief when he finally arrived at our new temporary abode. A little later and after my mother had a conversation with our street representative, my grandfather also started work with our new socialist friends. His reward: food for himself while on their site and a rucksack full of firewood every day. Firewood is an extremely important commodity. In towns, as a rule, you have gas or electricity, but not after a war of such dimensions. So you don't cook unless you have wood. Bomb sites had long been cleared of anything still burnable, furniture became redundant, people had started cutting branches off the street's chestnut trees. But we had wood and had constructed in the yard a kind of stove made from bricks collected from bombed-out buildings, of which there was fortunately an abundance. When we cooked, it was for everyone in the house. Everyone contributed and survival became easier when you practised all for one and one for all. We supplied the wood and potatoes, one person once supplied a whole jar of honey, everyone was always queuing somewhere for something. Once someone came away with a cupful of flour and on another occasion we acquired half a bucket full of green tomatoes pickled in salt. What a coup! Where they came from remained a mystery, we could not get any more. Apart from that we all went out looking for dandelions, sorrel, plantain, shepherd's purse, stinging nettles and if it was broad-leaved you took it anyway. Unfortunately, everyone looked for these greens and that is why they were so few and far between. The nicest nettles always grew on bomb sites, but in such dangerous locations that no one dared to go anywhere near them. No one but the most foolhardy would attempt to harvest them.

If someone tells you nowadays stinging nettles are delicious and healthy, they contain more of this and that than spinach, don't believe a word. It is foolish. If you are down to stinging nettles insufficiently cooked due to lack of firewood with nothing but water added, you will notice that you are not a herbivore and if you have nothing else to add to this weed it will be your death. In the long run and in the short run.

Then a novelty food came onto the market. It was called a bread roll. One bread roll distributed for every child at school. Looking back, it must have been part of a devilish plan to exterminate Germans. The bread roll looked bluish grey. It smelled rancid and bitter – a kind of soapy bitterness. It made you feel unwell and vomit. It was an emetic. Most children became quite ill and it was impossible to get used to the taste. It is actually your body's warning mechanism in action. It's saying: don't eat this. As so often happens, there is always someone who does not get ill. People like me for instance. The bread roll tasted awful, I felt uneasy about it, but I was not sick. I even ate the ones that other children gave away. They just could not keep them down. I may have done well on them, perhaps they would have poisoned me. I never found out. The bread rolls were withdrawn. There had not been enough flour to make these rolls to help starving children, therefore flour made from chestnuts had been added. The unfortunate choice had fallen on horse chestnuts. Hence the colour, the taste and the after-effect. My advice: unless you know you are a camel, don't eat horse chestnuts.

Then we had 'The People's Soup Kitchen'and those six open-ended tickets from the street representative. Open-ended meant no fixed date. We were entitled to six litres of soup per day. My grand-mother and I collected the soup in small one- and two-litre milk cans. The recipe for the soup was simple to follow, the same we had used under Hitler. I could easily have cooked it myself. There were hundreds of people in the queue. The main ingredient was therefore obvious: add another bucket of water, people are very hungry today. All food that could be produced was sent up to our new social-ist friends, what they rejected was used for the civilian population. It was unfortunate for the civilian population that the new social-ist friends could use everything, with few exceptions. Two of those exceptions were fish heads and cabbage stalks. Many, many years later my brother and I stood by the sea in North Wales looking out onto the waves and clouds in silence, as we often did, when he sud-denly turned to me and said: 'Do you remember Ludwigslust? We used to eat the raw rotten cabbage stalks. We were too hungry to wait for them to be cooked.' Yes, dear brother, I remember.

The fish heads and cabbage stalks were sent back to the peo-ple's soup kitchen, alas, no longer fresh. Then you had the choice between soup or fish heads no longer visible under swarms of flies. My grandmother had a good nose for what was still edible fish and what should be rejected. She always opted for fish if at all possible. With six tickets we were allowed two bags full of fish heads. They were crawling with maggots and the heads could have walked into our bags without our assistance. But my grandmother always helped them on their way with as many maggots as possible. On the way back she kept reminding me, 'Hold your bag tightly closed, child, all your maggots are getting out.' When we got back, the bags were immediately emptied into boiling water. It made a gelatinous soup, you ate it all and sucked the fish heads clean. And the maggots were, after all, almost pure protein made from fish heads.

Enjoyable as I found going to school, it posed considerable obsta-cles. School was unfortunately just beyond the compound of the *Kommandantura* – the official Russian head office of the new admin-istration. It also housed a lot of the staff's families, with quite a few children. These naughty little devils made it their business to wait for us as we went past the building on our way to school. They always had a good supply of stones on their side of the fence with which to pelt us as we ran by. There was nothing one could do about it. 'Take care you don't get hit,' said my mother and knowing me, added, 'Under no circumstances throw any stones back.' She made me promise. If it hadn't been for that, I would have clobbered those ghastly kids.

The change from the Hitler to the Stalin regime provided us with familiarity and continuity in the marching and the singing glorifying our leaders and their ambitions to make the world a better place. All the square bashing I had done to the tune of the Radetsky march had not been in vain. The Russians used the same marching style and whether I am number three or number seven or ten in a line, I can turn 90 degrees without getting out of step. Lines of ten were very popular and 10 x 10 looks very impressive. On special occasions you could easily get groups of 100 x 10 marching down the high street to the town hall or market square. School would close on such days and all shops closed, so the entire population did not miss the opportunity to hail a Party leader on the town hall balcony and to pay jubilant homage to some tin-pot politician making a speech somewhere.

Once I was chosen by my school to read out Lenin's curriculum vitae in Russian, before a Party mogul's speech of course. The well orchestrated applause was deafening and everyone was bowled over at the mere mention of Lenin or Stalin or Engels or Marx or Gorki. By the way, I like Gorki. The singing followed the same pattern that we were used to under Hitler, very loud before and after a speech, no change there then. The only difference was where before we had waved flags with the Hakenkreuz we now waved Hammer and Sichel, and instead of raising our right arm to just above shoulder height with an open hand, we now made a fist. And instead of singing *Deutschland, Deutschland über alles* we now sang *Wachet auf, Ihr Völker, der Verdammten,* (Arise, you wretched of the earth'), the Internationale. You could not risk being absent from these rather frequent events because officials were there, just like under the Nazis, with clapper boards calling out your name and when you answered '*hier*' they made a tick alongside your name. As if you would want to miss an opportunity to declare your devotion to and solidarity with the new regime and its aim to be the enlightened leader of the world!

After one of those glorious stage-managed events in which, of course, my entire school took part, my class and I, about 30 of us, of which 12 were boys, stayed behind and skylarked about in the market square. It was already dark, we laughed, played hide and seek, climbed lamp posts as one does, unsupervised and being 12 years old. We cheered some boys who had climbed a newly erected statue. Unfortunately, the statue was not safely anchored, it toppled over and its head broke off. Luckily, none of the boys was hurt. If it had been a statue of Cupid or some ancient Greek god it would not have mattered. But this had been a new statue of Lenin.

Attracted by the noise, the police arrived. Their station was also in the market place. All the boys were arrested, 11 of them, one had gone home earlier in the evening. All 11 were detained and accused of malicious damage to the statue of Lenin. My class was in a state of shock the following day, with only one boy present. Our 11 classmates, most only just 12 years old, were taken to court, accused not only of malicious damage but also of subversive and hostile actions against communism and without further delay the sentences were announced. 20 years hard labour for ten of them and 30 years hard labour for one of them. Because that one was decadent and you could tell that he was decadent because he came from a noble family and his surname had the prefix 'von' (von Bassewitz).

Justice had been swift and the perpetrators of such evil had been duly punished. The young lives of 11 boys aged 12 had been flushed down the toilet as a lesson to us all. I now became aware of quite a procession of court cases, all involving some kind of offence against the communist regime. I got the impression that our new socialist friends were teaching us through hands-on experience how to behave and when to leave well alone. The harsh judgements were chilling and achieved what may have been intended. The silence of the masses. The empty desks in my classroom stayed empty. No one changed seats, no one wanted to move into a friend's empty chair. We all felt subdued and deeply worried. The empty seats were a cry for help, but there was nothing that any one of us could do. I don't remember such trials under the Nazis. I think I may have been too young to pay attention to them and the grown-ups in my family would have shielded me from such gross injustices. I know that people and whole families disappeared overnight, just like my friend and her family who bizarrely 'moved house' overnight, hours before we were going to give our dance performance in their barn.

You did not have to be Jewish to disappear without even leaving a message. I realise now how close we had come to disaster when my mother had said 'all children like sweets.' With such statements you became a subversive collaborator, you undermined the teachings of your leader and you plotted the downfall of your nation. Punishable with death at least. I say at least because there was the fate of your family to be considered as well. You could not come to the assistance of anyone, if you did, you were tarred with the same brush. The best thing was not to put your head above the parapet and hope you would not get noticed. You lived in the hope that this way of life would not last forever. Something would happen to let you out of this prison where they specialised not just in mental torture; no, their aim was to destroy you completely. Unless you saw sense and sang from the same hymn sheet. And it is indeed possible to sing hymn after hymn, dozens of them, and still be an unbeliever. You could still pray for help. Would somebody please, please, get us out of here?

In the middle of this gloom and out of the blue, the door to our two rooms opened one afternoon and who stepped in? My hero uncle. The one who had some toes burnt off and later in a Russian winter had some more frozen off and who was taken prisoner at Monte Cassino, then was shipped to Oran and from there to California, near San Francisco. Some people are lucky. The atmosphere in his POW camp was strained as most of the POWs were Japanese and they had not endeared themselves to the Americans. The Germans were pre-ferred, you could say, by default. My uncle's time in the States was spent picking cotton, which he said was a surprisingly hard job. When the war was over he was discharged and sent back to the old country by ship via England. But instead of being sent home to Germany he and thousands of others were interned and distributed all over England to work on farms or elsewhere. He and his comrades were no longer POWs, they were now forced labour. While it is unethical to put POWs to work, it is almost unavoidable. When one country sends its men away to play soldiers, then who is going to replace the workforce to produce food and everything else to keep the country going? I remember, instead of working with German men on our farms, we were working with POWs. It is downright wrong to requisition men no longer POWs as forced labour, it is shameless exploitation of the helpless. Germany's victors debased themselves.

So, there he was, my uncle, in Great Britain on a farm near Tonbridge Wells for more than a year after the war with no hope of finding out what had happened to us all. He had heard that Germany east of the Oder had been cleared and he was sick with worry and could not wait for the day he would be released. The day came but before he and a few hundred others could board the ship, they were fleeced by their guards. A few small presents, such as a pen and a manicure set from San Francisco for me and some cocoa from the farmer's wife where he had worked, given to him as a farewell present, were stolen from him, as was done to everyone else. British fair play was not in evidence. My uncle had done no more than his duty when he was called up, he did not volunteer, he showed himself to be brave and selfless in times of extreme danger and now, thin and hungry, they got very little to eat in Britain, in ill health at the age of only 28, with clothes old, torn and dirty. With no home to go to, not knowing where his family was nor whether they were still alive, he found himself kicked off the island like unwanted rubbish. I am sorry to say that he called Britain '*Die Piraten Insel*' (the Pirate Island).

Like all the others before him he had walked to the Oder and was not allowed any farther. He was nearly out of his mind with fear as to what our fate might have been. Then, with information from the Red Cross, he walked to Ludwigslust, begging for food as he went. We were overcome when he stood there inside our room. My grandmother was there. I was there, my little sister, my little brothers. We recognised him and did not move. It was like a beautiful dream and you have to keep very still in case the dream fades away. Then my grandmother called out his name and they fell into each other's arms. My grandmother had shouted so loud that all the other people in the house came running upstairs wondering what had happened. I remember one woman from downstairs quietly asking my uncle: 'May I hug and welcome you home, because my son has stayed in Russia and will never come back.' My uncle said, 'That is hard' and he gave her the biggest hugs and kisses that any son could have given his mother. Like everything connected with this catastrophic war, even joy was tinged with sadness and a constant reminder never to forget your fellow human beings.

Neighbours arrived with little gifts of food to witness the unbelievable sight of a lost soldier who had come home. When my grandfather and mother came back from work that night there were silent hugs. Words could not express anyone's feelings and emotions. Talking about the kind of life, or shall I say the trials of life, since our last farewell years ago, came little by little in days and weeks to come.

After my uncle had recovered a little he went by himself to the Russian barracks to ask for a job. He was sociable, quite clever and adaptable, and to no one's surprise landed a job in the officers' quarters polishing their boots and keeping their uniforms tidy. A priceless job. It meant food for him, the officers gave him money and free salt.

You have no idea how valuable salt is, when there is none about for a long time. Once two Russian soldiers knocked on my grandmother's door offering a pair of shiny boots in exchange for some salt. And my grandmother said, '*Jungchens* – little boys – take the boots back to where you took them from, because you will be in trouble. They are your officer's boots, aren't they? I have some salt I can let you have and then go away.' They gratefully accepted the salt and left quickly. The ordinary soldier struggled.

We had regained another much loved member of our family. We were about to lose one. My brothers were very weak, as I have said before. Their little lives were spent mainly lying down and resting. My little sister, very frail and thin, used to be taken to school in a hand cart by my mother until she got the job with the Russian army. Thereafter, my grandmother took her to school in the cart and collected her again. My little sister was stubborn, she wanted to go to school. She was but a willo'-the-wisp but had such a lively and inquisitive mind that nothing would hold her back from satisfying her curiosity about the world, she just had to go. Music and singing were her great loves and she had such a silvery, clear voice, it matched her silvery hair and her shining grey-blue eyes. Now, I know, her eyes shone with fever. She was my light, always. She grew more and more fragile and instead of going to school, she spent her days lying on a sofa wrapped up in blankets.

One afternoon, I was left alone looking after her and my little brothers. My grandmother had gone out queuing for some food somewhere, the others were working at the barracks. I was sitting at a table opposite the sofa where she was lying, propped up on pillows, covered by a blanket and shivering in spite of the bright sun shining on her through the very large windows. A neighbour came in with a small gift of food on a saucer. A few luscious red raspberries. I was so happy. I had something to give to her. Precious food. I showed her the raspberries and didn't they look appetising and lovely? She did not seem to recognise me. I put the saucer within easy reach and somewhat confused, sat down on the chair opposite the table again. The table was pushed close to the sofa so that she should not fall off.

Her thin little hands moved restlessly over her blanket and she started singing with little strength to pronounce the words. It was a lullaby. I knew it well. Then she reached for the glowing red colours on the saucer and found they would fit on her fingertips, she laughed and covered all her fingers with these translucent red jewels, and she held her hands with the red thimbles close to her face, admiring the red rosy sparkle in the sunlight, no more recognising them as food, still humming and singing 'the flowering tree whispers as if in a dream, sleep, sleep, sleep tight, my little child.' Her mummy was not with her as she sang herself to sleep and it was a long time before I realised that her sleep was so deep that she would not ever wake up again.

I don't recall what happened that evening, everything was so disjointed. I was sitting in someone's garden under an apple tree, *Schöner von Boskop*. Funny what one remembers. I also remember my grandfather saying 'I never dreamt that one day I would have to make a cross for my grandchild's grave.' My mother sat with my little sister all night, she never cried and in the morning she stood up and went to work at the Russian barracks. To ask for a day off because your child was dying or had died was really not an acceptable excuse.

My sister's body was collected among a sea of flowers. On the day of her funeral so many people had arrived that most had to stay outside the chapel. Then, something threw me completely. Waiting outside the chapel were over 20 children, all dressed in white, accompanied by their parents, relatives and teachers, my little sister's classmates and friends. That was too much for me. I had last cried when I had bent over that young boy, beaten and with his throat cut in the snow on 14 February 1945. Now I cried again for the first time since that day. I seemed to cry for hours, thousands of hot tears in silence. My mother did not cry. A mother does not cry when she is all that stands between her children and the world.

A few days later a letter was delivered by a translator from the Russian *Kommandantura*, in Russian with a translation in German. The letter was from Vassili. He had shadowed us for more than a year. The letter expressed shock, sadness, care and love. My mother was looking for only one thing. Would he say 'If you had married me, she might still be alive.' No! Of course not! Vassili was not capable of such thoughtless cruelty. And my mother was relieved. If she had married him, he would have been the right one. And if I had become a little Russian girl I would have been so proud to have had him as my stepfather.

To lose my dearest sister after the worst was over was unimaginable. After all the heartbreak, the fear, the terror and sheer insanity that had held us in its claws, from which one could not reasonably expect to escape, the worst was my sister's death. Starvation got the better of her. And that in spite of the fact that our food had been enhanced with natural products, such as ground acorns and horse chestnuts, enriched with the vitamins and minerals from stinging nettles and a healthy salt-free diet!

My mother steadfastly refused to have my father declared dead. As a widow she would have been entitled to extra help, meaning extra food. This dilemma caused her great distress. After all, there were my poorly little brothers.

My grandparents and my uncle supported her. It took three grown-ups to work to procure just about enough food for two little boys and outside school hours I scavenged some food for my grandmother and myself. My grandparents did not care for their lives any longer. Their aim was to eat the minimum required to stay alive and qualify for the 800 calorie per day ration book. Although the 800 calories never materialised in full, what was available they gave to their grandchildren.

Another thing I remember, the fine smile of my grandfather when I showed him the rescued Goethe.

I, myself, was fortunately very hardy and as I had found solace in dancing during the harsh war years before, I now found myself in circumstances that turned my passion for dancing into sheer joy and hope.

Marching and singing, we dragged ourselves through another winter, 1946/47. Rumour had it that there was more food in the American, French and English sectors of Germany and people fled to the West whenever there was an opportunity. The Americans, in particular, were said to have not only nylons and cigarettes, people claimed that they had meals on every day of the week! Nylons and cigarettes you could just about believe. But eating seven days each week! Come off it! Well done, Yankees.

But it was not easy to go west. Borders had been put into place with proper border police. Moreover, it was made an offence to leave. By doing so, you declared war on communism, you became an enemy of the free and you well deserved to serve time in prison or in a gulag. Your children were taken away from you to be educated in community camps and made aware of the advantages of true socialism. They learnt: 'If I don't have a cow, I shall make sure my neighbour's cow gets poisoned.' To try to escape to the West was a dangerous undertaking. People were arrested by the hundreds, subjected to show trials and given harsh sentences as a deterrent to others. And still no word from my father.

TO THE BORDER

My grandmother reminded my mother of the address of our New York relatives. My mother did not want to know. There was by then so much anti-German hostility about that even with the best will people at large doubted that a German person could look like an ordinary human being with just one head, two arms and two legs. The vast majority of Germans were, in fact, just like me and my family, persecuted victims of fascism and now communism. Constantly under the threat of losing our freedom and even our lives unless we toed the line. You were manipulated like a puppet and if you failed to please your masters your string was cut. What the State or your leaders did was done with your explicit approval. You did not even have to approve of anything yourself. Your leader took the burden of this responsibility upon himself.

My mother decided that despite the obstacles and obvious danger she was going west with us children. If she didn't try she would most probably lose her remaining offspring to disease and hunger.

My grandparents would stay because the grave of my little sister was now in that town and my uncle would not move away from his parents. He never made it to the West even after my grandparents' death. My mother started planning. It should not be too difficult with a bit of cunning. Her, me and one thin little boy each. We would have to make it work. As if on cue a letter arrived. From my father. My mother virtually fainted. He had been released by the Allies almost two years after the war. He had been kept on as forced labour until it was no longer possible to get any work out of him. My father had been a big, tall man and now weighed 84lb and had no teeth left in his mouth.

In spite of that, he had fared better than others. He was a natural linguist and French was his preferred foreign language. He was also a great admirer of French culture and literature. During the war it was of great advantage to him, he had made so many friends in France and had to take great care not to openly fraternise with the enemy, an offence for which you would be shot as a traitor. Many years after the war one old gentleman, with whom he had been particularly good friends, died. And the family halted the funeral until they had traced my father through the Red Cross, so that he could attend.

I have strayed again. Back to the letter. My father now lived north of Hamburg in a small village in a large wooden hut. He had tried in vain to find us because his letters addressed to his sister in Berlin had been returned marked 'bombed out'. By the time he had arrived back in Germany the border between East and West had been closed. He could no longer get across like my uncle and was spared the walk to the Oder to be told 'so far and no farther'. It was again the Red Cross that matched our names against his search. There was no holding my mother back now. We wrote letters to my father every day but under no circumstances mentioned that we would try to get across the 'Black Border'. We knew that letters from East to West and vice versa were opened and spied on by the communist regime, as others to their grief had discovered.

At this stage I would like to say a few words about the two opposing ideologies representing East and West as they seemed to me as a

12-year-old child. Basically, I saw nothing wrong with the aims of the communist ideals, but the idea ran counter to human competitive progressive behaviour so the whole idea falls flat on its face. I could not see any progress there. I was all for going west.

And yet I saw glaring flaws in the Allied handling of post-war Germany. In my very young life, where any normality had been absent, I had become very critical and cautious about anything and everything. There was my uncle and then my father, two honest, hardworking, honourable, absolutely trustworthy and caring men, being kept behind as forced labour in a foreign country cock-a-hoop at having defeated evil Germany, including evil me. After the end of the war there was no such thing as a POW. There was only forced labour. But at the same time the Allies condemned Germany for having used POWs as forced labour during the war. This attitude did not go down well with me. It did not go down well with the vast majority of people, not then or now. Our victors came across as two-faced and not to be trusted. I feel sure that this was not the intention but this was a by-product of war and just one aspect of exultant victory. Nonetheless, without food you cannot live, so go where the food is; but always take it with a very big spoonful of caution and, sadly, mistrust. Pitiful my life, really.

Back to my mother's plan. How to get across the Black Border? We practised what to do and what to say should we get caught. It was to be a warm, sunny day. All four of us were to get dressed in skimpy old summer clothing: that was easy, no cardigan, which we did not have anyway, wearing old shoes, our only ones and about to fall to bits. We had no problem with our outfits. Our 'disguise' was honest and perfect. We looked the same as before! We would have a tin mug on a string round our waist and our mother would have a large bucket as well as a mug. Nothing on our heads and no protective garment of any kind, as we would not need it, because we were berry pickers, wild strawberries, raspberries, possibly mushrooms. We should have been back home by the evening but got lost in the forest.

My mother learned the map and villages near the border by heart and one day our grandmother accompanied us to the station to take a train for a village in a forest close to the border. My uncle and grandfather went to work as usual so as not to attract attention. When the train moved off we waved and my little brothers shouted with delight because we were off on such an exciting journey. I saw my darling grandmother cry and was fully aware of the seriousness of our undertaking. It was still very early in the morning when we arrived at the small village and ambled casually off into the forest. My mother was very confident. We picked berries as instructed, some mushrooms which could have been toadstools – for our purpose it did not matter. My mother rehearsed the boys for the umpteenth time in case we got separated and she kept us to the edge of the forest, so that we could see where we were. Above all, she was hoping to find a person who knew this area to ask which way to go. We were lucky, we met an old farmer with a scythe on the way to his field.

My mother stopped him. 'I have already lost one child due to starvation. I want to take my other three to the West, where do I go?' Her question was short and sweet. The farmer thought for a while, then said, 'Don't go. They will have you back at the police station in no time at all. But if you insist, go to the end of the forest with the sun on your left in this direction, you come to a meadow, beyond this is a cornfield, then open green ground, beyond this you find a line of bushes and willow, along this runs a small stream, the stream is the border. But be careful, the police have dragged them back from beyond the stream. You will only be safe if you continue in this direction and get onto a railway line. Once there, look north and you should see a building in the distance. That is the first station in the West. Only then are you safe. I hope I don't see all of you again.'

He put his finger to his lips. We understood and nodded our thanks. We moved carefully and silently towards the meadow through the wood. My mother whispered, 'Keep low, no talking, follow me.' I brought up the rear. As we approached the cornfield we heard suddenly the barking of a big dog. Presumably a German shepherd. We were not frightened of dogs, having grown up with Rottweilers and German shepherds. They were the preferred dogs of the border police.

'Quick,' hissed my mother, 'into the corn, lie down and don't move.' We did, out of breath and with pounding hearts. We were in danger alright. Just don't panic.

Ahead of us several well armed border guards were passing with two German shepherds. We stayed in our spot for quite some time. The guards came back after about forty minutes from the left and then back again twenty minutes from the right. We waited for this to be repeated twice, then made our move when they departed to the left. Still ducking, we ran for the willow trees, there was the stream – and then disaster struck.

The whole area was a morass. My mother sank in to her knees, unable to get out. The two of us were so attuned to the constant danger we had been exposed to for such a long time and I was so independent and resourceful that without any words I ushered my brothers across over broken stems and branches to the other side, well away from the stream. I told them to lie down in the grass, don't move and shut up or your big sister will wallop you. This was meant to be reassuring.

I rushed back to my mother. I broke off lots of willow branches and arranged them like a platform around my mother. Between the two of us we had almost managed to get out of the sump when we heard the returning dogs. We freed ourselves with our last bit of strength and made it over the water into the meadow where the grass swallowed us up. The guards returned laughing and talking past the area where we had got stuck, the dogs pulled forwards on their short leashes, their noses did not detect us. We were covered with blackish, somewhat sweet smelling water and peat, which must have disguised the scent. As we made a dash to where I had hidden the boys we heard the sound of a train in the not so far distance. We ran for it. The train had gone but to our immense relief we were now walking on the sleepers of a railway line and about one kilometre ahead of us was the building, as the farmer had said, the railway station. My mother took the boys by their hands and almost ran for the station. I fell more and more behind, it really had been too much. I felt exhausted and faint. When my mother turned round to see where I was I must have been nearly 300 metres behind her. She waved to me and shouted 'I will come back,' and then she ran, carrying my smallest brother. she made it to the station, dropped off the boys and then returned to help me.

It is funny, the thought that went through my head then. If the border guards had followed me to snatch me back, what would have been best? Should my mother have come back? Then all four of us would have been lost. If she continued to run away with the boys, she would have saved two out of her four children. And I remember thinking, 'It's alright, mother, I quite understand.'

In later life I often thought back to us on that railway line. There we were, debilitated, hungry, dispossessed, rags for clothes, not a penny to our name, no home to go to, escaping from the jaws of death; but we were the ones that built Germany up again with its *Wirtschaftswunder*. The only good German is a dead one? I will show you!

Back to the station. People there were surprised. Single men had made it to the West. But they had never seen a woman with three children succeed. We were all given a drink of water. A local farmer was called. He kindly took us in his horse-drawn cart to the nearest camp. We really could walk no more. The camp was quite something, huge tents, no beds, not much space on the floor to lie down, only benches along the rough tables, and hundreds and hundreds of destitute people. All like us: pitiful figures. Volunteers with armbands displaying *Sanitäter* or Red Cross walked round, taking names of new arrivals or carrying away those that had fainted or collapsed. Every newcomer was given two meal tickets per day. Meals were served all day, a piece of bread and the traditional water soup. You could have either two meals straightaway or have one in the morning and one in the evening. We had two meals straightaway. We knew from experience, if there is food, eat it immediately. Who knows what will happen later.

My mother asked the Red Cross to send a message to my grandparents to say we were safe and a message to my father with more details to follow about where exactly we were. The Red Cross transferred us in one of their vehicles to a camp in Hamburg. The camp consisted again of benches and tables, no beds for lack of space. Again, there were hundreds and hundreds of people. The police worked round the clock, relaying messages to relatives. That is how my father heard where we were to be found. It took him another day to get money together from villagers near his camp to pick us up from Hamburg.

In spite of all the hardships, people always clubbed together to help some other unfortunate person out of a sticky patch. No one ever wanted the money back. I will never forget that wonderful day when we were slumped on our benches in that vast tent in Hamburg when this strange and yet so familiar person walked towards us with this big, heartwarming smile on his face. He called out my mother's name. It was Daddy! We hugged and kissed him so much that we nearly suffocated him. We were a little family again. Quite a rarity after the war. Five out of six still alive. But my little sister missing.

To put the figures into perspective; we were indeed an anomaly. Out of the 26 closely related members of our large family that were in our house on 13 February 1945, only nine were still alive. The others had died, been murdered or had committed suicide.

We arrived in high spirits and with so much hope in our new home. Home was a hut. There were over 100 huts. We shared that hut with five other parties. The men had sectioned it off into six individual living spaces. There was us and a young couple from Tschechoslowakia who had lost all their family plus their only child. Then there was a middle-aged couple who had lost both their boys in Russia, then one set of grandparents who had lost all but three of their grandchildren and one man, alone, he had lost all. There was also a single woman, I don't know anything about her, she died shortly after our arrival. That was home from home now, no money, no ration cards, two stools, one table, no beds but straw donated by the villagers to sleep on.

We started with emergency ration cards and some money given to us by the village mayor. I also remember one loaf per week as a gift from the local baker and 125gm of margarine per week from the village shop. Local people held a collection for us for pots and pans, plates and some linen. One local woman gave me a bucket and invited me into her garden to see the rabbit and then she took the rabbit's aluminium plate away and gave it to me. The rabbit had to eat from the floor boards, but I had my own plate. This plate is still a family treasure. We also have from my father a mug, which he crafted like some prehistoric man out of a tin plate, cutting it into shape with stone tools. He even gave it a handle with the edges turned in for a smooth finish. It was water tight. My father thinks this mug saved his life: there was so little to eat, but sometimes kind people would give you a drink and in that part of the world you cannot drink water but wine. Water is far too contaminated. Two litres of wine in drips and drabs per week can make all the difference. But first of all you must have a mug into which the wine can be poured. And my father had clever hands.

From a Swedish organisation we received clothes and shoes, but none my size. We also received from another charity one bread roll per day, this time without horse chestnuts, it was a rather small bread roll, but much appreciated. I believe this was paid for by the American taxpayer. We also received one 500ml bottle per week of unrefined cod liver oil per family. I do not know who paid for this. I want to say a very big thank you to the countries and the people who made these gifts to Germany, it was so heartening to be able to think that not everyone thought we ought to be put down merely because we were German.

When it was warm, I walked barefoot and saved my shoes for bad weather. Once I had to walk for a long distance, someone had offered us some eggs and they had to be collected. Someone's brother lent me his shoes for the day, they fitted me. I learned life from the bottom up. It was hard and there were divisions between people. There are people that have no shoes, and then there are some people that have shoes for some of the time and in the top league there are people that can call shoes their own seven days a week. My resolution for the future was to own shoes for every day of the year, all the time. I had to work unusually hard for my living.

There was school. My brothers could go to the local school for the time being. My school was, of course, in the next town, 12 kilometres away again! As we did not have enough money for the train ticket, it was Shanks's pony for me. On top of it all, my mother had me put into a class one year above my age. She felt I had missed so much, I should learn a bit faster and work a bit harder. I certainly did.

School hours were in two shifts. One week from 8.00 to 13.00, the next week from 14.00 to 19.00. The teachers worked double shifts for single pay. There were few teachers and very large classes. Our teachers were determined to get into our heads what we had missed during the Nazi and post-war years. During lessons you could have heard a pin drop. There were only five minutes between lessons, barely time to go to the toilet. We struggled with a shortage of books, only a few scraps of paper to write on and where does one get pens from? Once I was lucky. I was given a toilet roll. I used it for geography, with Ireland starting on page 87.

No one wanted my Russian. There was a lack of specialist teachers, so it was not even on the timetable. I could have read and translated to them articles from *Pravda*, or Gorki or Pushkin. Instead I struggled with English and French. I was thrown in at the deep end, my class was reading Maupassant and *The Little Prince* by Antoine de Saint-Exupery. In English we read *The Canterville Ghost*, what a laugh, and then there was *Hamlet*. Oh, I loved *Hamlet*, particularly the part of Ophelia. I could, surprisingly, hold my own in Latin, thanks to my outstanding first teacher. After *veni, vidi, vici* I progressed finally to *Gaudeamus igitur*. I finished school and proved myself in my chosen, very unusual profession.

My father and brothers recovered slowly; it took them years to be classed as reasonably fit. My mother was thin and wiry, but still she kept going. We were later rehoused by the government in Stuttgart. There were millions of Germans living like us in substandard huts, barracks and improvised camps. There was no proper sanitation, the water stand pipe always a long way away from your hut, and keeping living quarters warm was a constant worry. The families in our camp were allocated three tree stumps each in the forest surrounding the camp, to cook with and keep warm. Very good and thank you very much. But three stumps do not keep you going through a winter. So, we were all digging the third stump. The forester used to come along on his bike. 'Good morning, Mr Brown, still digging your third?' 'Good morning, oh, it is you? Yes, still digging my third.' The forester was a good man and his vision was poor. He never saw that a good hectare of mature pines had disappeared in order to get at the third. Well, no country can move forward living like this.

CLIMBING OUT OF A DARK HOLE

Millions were relocated. No one could choose the town or area they wanted. The announcement was made to us at our camp that the town of Stuttgart would take 20,000 displaced people that autumn from this or that area and the trains would leave on such-and-such a date. The camp would be closed the day after. And the move took place with military precision. Our limited possessions were picked up by lorry, driven to the appropriate railway station and off you went on the same train. You were duly picked up, again by lorry, at your destination and driven to your new home. The town was ready for you. Accommodation was invariably in flats. But what flats! The style and colours were superior. The area overlooked the river Neckar. Stuttgart old town was situated within the lower reaches of the Neckar valley, with heat in summer often over 40°C and with the humidity from the river it could be somewhat oppressive. The landscape was park-like, with vineyards everywhere, play areas for small children within sight of the mother's kitchen window, a few steps away from the front door, meaning lots of play areas with sand pits, paved areas with coloured stones so that you could play games on them, and benches around the games areas for those that just wanted to watch.

Chess was very popular, the carved pieces as big as small children were kept in wooden boxes alongside the games area. When you finished your game, you put the pieces into the box, locked them with a proper lock and you would hang the key on a hook under the overhanging lid. Some chess areas had viewing platforms, because the area was so large and the figures so big that you lost track of where you were and when you were ready to make your move, you would climb down the stairs and pick up your knight or rook and manhandle it to its new position. It was great fun and very popular. There were so many play areas and such a variety of sports fields, sports halls and swimming pools such as I have never seen in the UK. And so many schools, so close together. Where did they get all the pupils from? Firstly, class sizes in Germany are much smaller than in Britain. Fifteen pupils is the maximum number for the first few years. The area where we lived in Stuttgart was exclusively populated by families expelled from their homes east of the Oder-Neiße line, now the border between Germany and Poland. To me, this is just Europe and that is how it should be.

We were allocated a second-floor flat consisting of three large rooms, a kitchen, fully equipped, toilet and shower, a huge balcony, the stairwell and stairs partially of concrete and Italian marble, all window sills of Italian marble. The huge kitchen sink was also of Italian marble and the windows double-glazed of a standard not seen in some countries more than fifty years later. There was an extremely generous attic space for each party living in the flats, so you could leave your spare furniture somewhere; and as no one had spares, we just had the space. A separate drying area in the loft was also available, in case it was raining when you had your wash day. Downstairs was a very large communal storage area for bikes or motor bikes; no one had any of these either, so the area was used for prams, children's tricycles and the like.

Each party had two separate lock-up cellars, one for hobby work and one for storage. Wine, for instance, potatoes, preserves, and so on. In Germany the milkman does not call, the wine man calls. On one day of the week stacks of crates would stand by the front doors, two crates of such-and-such a wine, one or two crates of this or that beer, for children one or two crates of Malzbier, fruit juice, Erdbeer Sekt, Apfel Wein (which is not cider) and so many other drinks. In the evening, when you came back from work, you would carry it all down into the cellar. If your front door was in full sun, 40°C plus, very common in Stuttgart, you would give your key to a neighbour to kindly move the crates into the cool cellar. I never heard of a stolen crate.

To us it felt like climbing out of a dark hole into civilisation. But now, in spite of the modernisation of these flats, no Germans live there any more, they moved away. The flats are now lived in by asylum seekers and I hope they are as happy as we were then and that they will be able to build a new and better life for themselves. I wish them happiness and success. At the time of writing, the authorities have started to rebuild the entire area, about the size of a town of 20,000 or so. Where we lived is a gigantic building site. New flats and houses have gone up already. If you live in a house in Germany built after the war, now 50 years old or so, beware, the bulldozers are just around the corner.

By the way, the brand-new property that had belonged to my relatives who had had their dog Hasso shot was, after the expulsion of Germans from the East, given to a Polish couple who, after their death, left the property in their will to the son of these relatives. He had survived the war and was then living in West Germany. He in turn gave it officially as a gift to the heirs of the deceased Polish couple. A generous and noble gesture by both parties.

To rehouse millions of drifting homeless, hopeless Germans after the war in industrial areas like Stuttgart was brilliant, not just the execution of the plan but the whole idea was farsighted. Industry needed building up, jobs had to be created and translated into money-earning enterprises, which needed the creation of high-quality schooling, apprenticeships and further education. People had to know there would be a reward when they reached what they were aiming for. Your aim was to be better, and if you were better at something than everyone else then you knew what to do: be even better. It worked for the country. It worked for the individual as well.

When we arrived in Stuttgart, times were hard. My father was, quite frankly, unfit for work, apart from needing extensive dental work. The loss of his teeth had been due to scurvy. Both my parents were initially unemployed and walked, taking shortcuts, once a week 18km to the unemployment office in Stuttgart Bad Cannstadt. It took them all day. They never used a Pfenning for a tram. Everything was spent on us children. Once my father was offered a job that required a lot of walking; he quietly took his shoes off and put them on the counter. 'Alright, alright,' said the man behind the desk, 'I will find you something better next week.' He did. My father landed a job with the well-known international industrial giant Siemens and advanced to a senior position in years to come.

My brothers had to work very hard at school. They had been left far behind and were feeble little skeletons. But they did very well and I admired their tenacity. The German government rewarded success at school. For every grade one you got, you were paid 20 DM per month and for every grade two you earned 10 DM per month. You got nothing for grade three. Grades one and two were suddenly very hard to achieve. But the boys and I managed to earn more money than my parents were paid in unemployment benefit per month. I actually bought a pair of shoes for my brothers on the never-never and proudly paid them off at 2 DM per month. The money from the government was, of course, paid to the parents, but it was good to know that without me there would have been no shoes. Both of my brothers gained engineering degrees and were able to buy their own houses while their children were still at school.

But I suffered. The boys had been too small to remember the cruel details of the end of the war and the years after. My mother and I had always shielded them, covering their heads with clothes or blankets when we did not want them to see something. We said it was too cold, keep under cover. I, the big sister, had to be alert, therefore. I had to see and then decide what I did not want them to see. And from my mother I learnt to be mother hen to them as she was to me. But I was already too grown up to be deceived and the memories would not go away.

Once I visited Monte Scherbelino in Stuttgart. *Scherben* means shards. This is a hill created out of the rubble of the bombed-out buildings and turned into a memorial site to commemorate the dead. The people who suffered under the dictatorships of Hitler and Stalin could do little to free themselves from their scourge. Many tried valiantly and found nothing but death. Their families were often murdered. Would you risk a heroic action knowing that your children, parents and other relatives would have to pay the price for your noble deeds? Suddenly the noble deed is no longer so appealing.

Well, there I was, looking down at beautiful Stuttgart, the pearl of the Neckar, the town I had come to love, natural beauty tinged with sadness for me. Once it was the song *Märkische Heide*, embracing my homeland, now I was touched by Karl Gerok's poem, *'Da liegst du nun im Sonnenglanz Schön, wie ich je dich sah, In deiner Berge grönem Kranz Mein Stuttgart, wieder da. Liegst da vom Abendgold umflammt Im Tale hingeschmiegt, Gleich wie gefaßt in grönem Samt Ein göldnes Kleinod liegt.'* 'There you lie resplendent in evening light/As lovely as I ever did see/Your mountains a green wreath around you/My Stuttgart, there again/You lie, bathed in flames of evening gold/Nestled in the valley/Just like a golden gem/Encased in green velvet.'

I felt sad and could not throw off the past few years. I looked at people, at landscapes, at lives through the eyes of the dead, my constant companions. I thought back to the traumatic day when we had been chased out of our house, out into ice and snow, without mercy. We were mere specks of life, far too lowly to be given a place in anyone's conscience. For us to exist was inconvenient for them. It had been 13 February 1945 when we were thrown out. By coincidence, the night of the Dresden firebombing. The utterly irresponsible, pointless, callous destruction of the embodiment of Europe. A deed done after the war was, to all intents and purposes, over.

There were bombings of towns by Germany and by the Allies in a form of senseless and vicious tit for tat. What was to be achieved? Dominance? Dominance over what? Defence? Defending what? To gain material wealth? People get that by working together, not by making war. To gain freedom? Or defend freedom? Whose freedom? Freedom from what or freedom for what?

My thinking on this topic comes across as silly. To expand my thoughts perhaps makes me seem even more silly. It all starts with a bully who has just one desire: to subjugate other living things. Such a bully is highly intelligent, manipulative, unscrupulous and successful. Why successful and how? They are very persuasive with carefully calculated, deceitful arguments aimed at strengthening and enhancing their position, while relying on the ignorance and gullibility of the masses. Masses can be manipulated. It is worryingly easy. One of the easiest ways is to keep people poor, ignorant and wanting. It is the wanting that is exploited and drives people down the wrong, well-illuminated, path. The persecuted and persecutors become one body leading to only one thing: destruction. To point a finger and say 'I did it, because you did it first,' is no defence. The European world got hopelessly lost in 1939 like this and it lasted for decades. Hatred and revenge blurred rational thinking.

Nothing could be gained nor influenced by the bombing of Dresden. It would not alter the outcome of the war in any way. The original number of inhabitants of Dresden had more than doubled by 1945, the town was overflowing with refugees, evacuees, orphaned and lost children. An additional 80,000 children had been registered in Dresden in 1945. By the way, the town was also overflowing with valuable rare breeds, such as horses. Hannoveraner, Lippizaner, Arabians and Trakehner. All had been transported to Dresden for safekeeping. Dresden was considered safe and for that reason had only minimal defences.

After the war the number of dead was agreed with the Allies not to have been more than about 40,000. The bombing of Dresden was a grave error. Dresden sank into ashes in just a few short hours, pointlessly, senselessly. Air force personnel taking part probably believed they were involved in a heroic battle. They were shamelessly misused by their governments. Burning alive thousands of children is nothing to be proud of. I have lived in Great Britain now for about 50 years. Show me the British person, or any person from any part of the world, that would do such a thing. You will not find one (the insane excluded). These air force personnel had been manipulated and brainwashed to commit a war crime. The indiscriminate bombing of the civilian German population was official British war policy as formulated and carried out by Winston Churchill. A crime against humanity for which some have been hanged, but not all. To make this policy acceptable to the British public it was sometimes rephrased as 'de-housing the German population'. A neutral observer might describe it as 'the burning alive of tens of thousands of children'.

German record keeping is usually quite good and original figures claim the death toll to have been 240,000 at least. Having experienced burning towns myself, I believe that a quarter of a million dead that night could be right. What sort of transport would you have had to have in place to ferry about one million people out of town in approximately 30 minutes? There was no safety in a cellar. You cannot sit out a firestorm. What sort of temperatures would your lungs be able to cope with? 40, 60, 200, 600 degrees Celsius? You would be dead before you worked it out.

Was Dresden a trial run for Hiroshima and Nagasaki? What was the thinking behind it? The argument seems that by burning a mere 100,000 people, chances are that most will be children, you save the lives of 50,000 or so military personnel. Atomic power is awesome. Once demonstrated you will not have to explain its destructive force in words, the spectacle of such an explosion is pretty convincing. To show it off effectively, did it really have to be dropped over two densely populated towns? Something is wrong here.

In my opinion, Dresden, Hiroshima and Nagasaki, these three towns will go down in history as examples of war crimes.

Murdering 6 million Jews is unbelievable. But evidence shows it is true. Apart from the Jews themselves, no one can be more devastated by it than the German people. It was committed under their very noses, although it was not publicised. I believe that my mother and my grandfather, without reservation, had no idea that these unspeakable crimes were taking place. I know of no one in my family who could have only remotely guessed what was going on. At the Nuremberg trials I believe it was Albert Speer who said, 'If 80 million have no access to a radio, then they will know nothing.' It was claimed that these murders were carried out in the name of Germany. This means: in my name. Would you do such a thing? Would your family do it? Of course not. I should not dare even to put this question to you because I know without doubt, you would not. But likewise, why would you think that I would do it? My family, my relatives, my friends would do it? I equally know without doubt that I and they would never do it.

I was getting quite morose and fretful. I had questions, questions and no answers. The worst of it was that I remembered things that happened in 1945. Quite trivial things would prompt my memory, perhaps the colour of a cardigan worn by someone walking down the street. Once, while waiting for a tram, I noticed a little boy and the way he tilted his head. That would suddenly bring back memories that I thought I had forgotten. I was nowhere safe. In 1945 I was frozen with terror. I looked, I saw, I walked past it and consigned it to the farthest and darkest corner of my mind. But now I started to thaw out and the world became hellish. I had to get away from it.

TO ENGLAND

One sunny spring day I arrived in London, at Victoria Station. I asked my way through to my green line coach stop and waited for No. 708 to take me to a town just north of London. I was surprised how well I understood English and how easily people understood me. My school English was not too bad after all. I was relieved. But while I was waiting, something else surprised me. I knew I was in a very important, prominent and famous part of London. Close to Buckingham Palace, Green Park, Westminster and the Houses of Parliament. I was not in the least prepared for what I saw. I felt myself transported back to scenes and images that I associated with the 1920s. I was, of course, never part of that decade. The cars, buses, all vehicles in fact, were so old fashioned, people were so colourlessly dressed, all of it looked so quaint, fragile, amusing in its strangeness and yet quite endearing, even lovable. Yet, and I almost feel apologetic about saying this, a curious doubt crept into my mind. Is this environment 'workable'? Can this work well for the country and its people? Well, I would find out.

Since that first day I have visited London very often – I didn't live far away. All the famous sights, I have been there: museums, parks, theatres, Madame Tussaud's, the Tower, Kew Gardens, hardly an underground station or trip by boat that I missed. But what I did not see were large areas of destruction. Kilometre upon kilometre of wasteland, ruins as far as your eyes could see. I had, of course, heard of the Blitz. But to my eyes it looked so small-scale. Yes, some areas were completely flattened, you would expect that after a bombing raid, but not to the extent I was used to. My comments may sound quite glib, ill informed, superficial, perhaps even irreverent. I am really sorry for this and don't want to hurt your feelings. But I was happy and very pleased with my decision to live in another country for a while. I did not know then that I was going to stay. I found some peace for myself and breathed a sigh of relief when I had not thought of this or that gruesome incident for three or four days. In Germany I had been so haunted by the terror of war and the post-war years under foreign occupation every day.

I never became part of this new country and its people. Here is how the separation began. It happened on one of the first few days in my new residence. At breakfast one day, toast was served and my colleagues cut the crusts off and discarded it. The crust was too hard. I was mesmerised by this procedure among the general chatter and laughter. There was food that was deemed inedible. A gulf opened between me and my new companions. It was a defining moment in my life in this country. I deliberately tried to be friendly and sociable but the gap between myself, a survivor of Zhukow's army, and the rest of the world was too wide to be bridged. I lived my life along-side people, no longer with people. I was tolerant of my companions' unthinking easy come, easy go approach to life, but I never felt at ease with them.

Sadly, mindless anti-German feeling ran high in the UK for quite a number of years after the war and was kept well alive by the trash served to its people by the government. The people looked at the world through its prescribed rose-tinted glasses and they saw themselves as noble and far superior human beings. Quite unlike Nazis like me.

This brought unexpected advantages. For instance, when I entered a common room with so many people in it that there was standing room only, the lively conversation stopped, they looked at me, then at one another and virtually all of them would demonstratively get up, walk out and while sailing past me gave me an icy stare. I always managed to keep a straight face, trying hard to suppress a laugh and then I made for a comfortable easy chair next to the fire, which would otherwise never have been vacated for me. While I was enjoying the warmth, the others now stood in a draughty corridor wagging their tongues. I was actually training as a nurse then and my company were all members of the 'caring profession'. I felt that after all I had experienced, nursing was a worthy profession for me.

Usually there were just two girls left, looking very embarrassed and most apologetic and trying so hard to explain the possible reason for the childish behaviour of the others. I begged them not to take it upon themselves to apologise for others. It was firstly not their fault that the others had debased themselves. Secondly, they were not responsible for the brainwashing of people at large and thirdly, I was not even offended. But these two girls were a tremendous boon, supportive, kind-hearted, highly intelligent and capable of thinking for themselves. We became friends. They became my family in England.

But one has to be on one's guard. I always was. Caution and distrust had become my second nature after experiencing such hostile behaviour. Little nasties were lying in wait for me ready to try to beat me up. When it came to racial abuse I was far worse off than people from Jamaica. Xenophobia was rife in Britain at that time. I well remember the signs that said 'no Irish, no dogs, no blacks'. Two of my new colleagues were young Jamaicans, very gentle and too afraid to leave the nurses' home. One day they even asked me to get them a bar of chocolate from Woolworths. They did not dare to go by themselves as they feared the verbal abuse and often were not even served in shops because they were black. I was really sad for them. If they had been German they could never have made it in England at that time. As a German I always ran the risk of ending up in a fight.

On one occasion I was confronted by three of my fellow students, hiding in a stock room. What can I say? Does one call it a tragic or a comical situation? I had been in quite a few scuffles with Russian and Polish soldiers and won. If a tart causes too much trouble, go and find another. When I am forced to fight I go for it all out. When I fight, I fight. I don't resort to minor blows. And these silly little no-hopers thought they could beat me up. They were lucky I let them go. I pulled off their caps, crunched them up and put them in my pockets. Then I invited them to see Matron and explain it all. They declined my offer. And you cannot see Matron if not properly dressed anyway. After that particular fight I was left alone. It did not pay to have a bust-up with me. I was awfully friendly and polite to them thereafter. Mockery takes on many forms.

My new colleagues reached their lowest point during my first Christmas in this country. I had half a day off on Christmas Eve. I had a very small Christmas tree and was happily settled with all my letters and had lit a few tiny candles on my tree, as is the German tradition. There was a knock on the door. It was a deputation representing all who lived on the same corridor as me − eleven of them. The message was this: they did not want to share their corridor with a Nazi. Downstairs was a free room. Would I move downstairs! Oh yes, of course, with pleasure. I did not wish to share a corridor with them and within half an hour I had transferred my belongings from upstairs to downstairs. I relit my candles and opened a bottle of Chateauneuf du Pape. This was such a hilarious situation that I can still giggle about it to this day whenever I think of it. What sort of thoughts were lurking in their brains? Basically, they did not know what a Nazi looked like and it could have been so easily resolved. All they had to do was to look into a mirror.

I would emerge from these situations as pristine as a duck from water because I was by then used to life with all sorts of people. Some of the worst are blinkered nationalists. Did these people think they could frighten me? I am not afraid of the devil. Neither have I become a respecter of titles, nor traditions, nor authority. But I am a respecter of life.

Sadly, due to racial prejudice it was rather difficult for me to secure better paid positions. It did not matter that I was better qualified with a better track record than other British applicants, as a rule I lost out. On one occasion it was taken to extremes. A sympathetic acquaintance of mine on the interviewing panel reported back to me that, although I was the favourite to land the job, the chairperson had objected: while the other applicant also spoke German, at least she was not German. I shed no tears. I could not have worked with these hypocrites. This bias, of course, affected and reduced my earning. This was a continuous worry because, due to rather tragic circumstances, I had to bring up my children on my own. Nonetheless, I managed. I always look forward and up, and I even sit on my own patch of land again, but this time it is the size of a postage stamp.

Some British customs and traditions amaze me. I was constantly told that Germans live and breathe uniforms. Never! We were forced to wear uniforms of one kind or another under Hitler and we loathed it. In Britain I was stunned to see that virtually everyone sported a uniform. And most people seem to like it. Children are sent off to school in uniform, even grown-up pupils, the 17-, 18- and 19-year-olds, some engaged, some house hunting, young ladies and gentlemen are forced to wear school uniform. Nursery school children wear uniform. That really takes the biscuit.

I was outraged when I had to buy school uniform for my first two children for the first time. I had an above average salary then, but the uniform cost me one and a half month's salary without the sports gear. I find it odd that clothes are rated higher in this country than knowledge. Parents are forced to spend their hard-earned money on outfits rather than books and other educational aids. Worse still, being uniformed and under the cosh of the education authorities, the children never learn to work things out for themselves. When they have grown up, tell them the NHS is free and they believe it. Critical thinking is not encouraged. The connection between paying taxes and what you can rightly expect for it in return is lost. No one seems to realise that you are entitled to education whether you turn up at school in an evening dress or rags. Your right to education does not depend on the clothes you wear.

Great Britain has no constitution. Are you surprised? I am surprised you don't know. The politicians know, but prefer not to say so. No one owns up to this fundamental shortcoming. Power stays with those that manage to keep the public ignorant. Sometimes, the great 'unwritten' British Constitution is mentioned. The unwritten British Constitution is worth as much as an unwritten driving licence. Fat lot of good that will do you. Britain was one of the countries that insisted that Germany had a proper constitution after the Second World War based on the American one. The German constitution is world class thanks to the British and the Americans – and it is written. The British politicians thought it was good enough for foreigners but the same politicians did not think that it was necessary for the British people to have one. Apparently, British politicians do not consider British people worthy of a constitution.

I worry about all this. I have grown up under Hitler and know only too well how quickly disaster can strike. What was Hitler's majority when he was elevated to power in Germany? 28 to 31%? That is first past the post voting. Less than one third of the country's voters then decide its destiny. The majority is silenced. That is dangerous and I have become so mistrusting. I do not feel safe. Nor are the British people safe. It takes one hiccup, one great depression like 1929 for instance. All sorts of splinter parties will emerge and right and left wing crackpots will all be jostling for power.

I have brought this subject up earlier: does this country work well for its people? In my opinion no, it does not. My children live here. They deserve better. The British people deserve better. Forget the nationalists and the treatment they have handed out to me and many other 'foreigners'. They will never learn. The vast majority of the British are warm-hearted and caring and have shown me great sympathy and real friendship. I am very thankful to them and I count myself lucky to be living among them.

I have seriously considered accepting British nationality. On studying the relevant papers though, I felt I could never voluntarily be someone's subject, neither can I swear allegiance to a person. In the end the deciding issues were these: now, seventy years after the war, commemorative services are held in many countries and towns. One of the towns is Danzig. The Second World War started with Danzig. Hitler reclaimed it for Germany and that was the start of the invasion of Poland. Since when was Danzig Polish? And was the area, called the Polish Corridor, not German as well? Danzig and Stettin have always been German. They had been part of the Hansa for hundreds of years.

In 1919 Danzig and the Polish Corridor – a new name for an entirely German area for more than one thousand years – were given in the Versailles Treaty to Poland. The German people there, like my relatives, might not have been all that displeased about Hitler's invasion. They may even have thought 'What took you so long?' There are always two sides to a story. The same applies to the Rhineland. Whose Rhineland was it? Was it not Germany's? And what about the people that lived in these parts of the country? Had they been asked whether they wanted to be Polish or French? Had they agreed? I am afraid the answer is no. That makes for trouble; if not straightaway, trouble will come later. And who was responsible for that? The statesmen who worked out the peace after the First World War. They were as ignorant, as arrogant, as stupid as the German Kaiser after the 1870/71 war with France. Totally inept at the job they were doing.

There was discontent for similar reasons all around Germany's new borders and resentment over this within the country itself. Nationalists, subversives and terrorist organisations began to flourish; add poverty to this and promises of a better life preached by revolutionaries – Hitler was only one of them but backed by Hindenburg – and it is easy to see that this can have no good ending. Insanity began to reign. It was Germany's most desperate and lamentable fate to ignite the last war amid this fermenting unrest, poverty, frustration, oppression, hopelessness. And it dragged millions upon millions of innocents to their undeserved deaths. Like me, like my family, my relatives, my friends and like yours. We were dragged into a maelstrom over which we had no control; so many had their minds poisoned and so many died as a result.

I do not under any circumstances accept excuses for atrocities committed by soldiers or others, including rape, which may or may not have left their victims alive. Some have said that soldiers have seen so much horror, one must excuse them. No. One must not! There is no excuse! If that were so, then I, after all that I have witnessed, would be justified in exterminating the entire human race. And yet I would not hurt anyone without just cause or reason.

Germany is sincerely mourning its past and feels the deepest regret for all the deaths and suffering caused. A country that has suffered so much itself fully understands the heartbreak of others.

But I ask myself, is there any regret felt by other countries for the completely unnecessary suffering they inflicted upon Germany? I only notice condemnation of Germany. A statue has been erected to commemorate Bomber Harris. The bomb that destroyed the Möhnetalsperre (a dam) was an engineering feat and engineering is highly rated in Germany; it drowned many people and even more cows. But it did not adversely affect the Ruhr industry. It was the wrong *Talsperre* (dam), it supplied mainly agricultural land. The British were never told this fact by their government; but they erect a statue anyway. And there was Dresden …

The main thing that tipped the scales against my assuming British nationality was my consternation and anger about post-war distortion of historical facts, which seems to have only one aim – to show the German people in as bad a light as possible. Britain was not the only country that engaged in this shameful practice.

For instance, Hitler did not invade my area of Germany and he did not annex my town. My home town would have celebrated its 1000th anniversary in the 1970s. My town was always German occupied from before the year 1000. The term Prussia was then generally applied to what was later termed Germany. Frederick the Great was not King of Germany but King of Prussia, with the Mark Brandenburg and Berlin at its heart. Before 1945, Prussia was Germany's what you might call largest and most important 'county'.

Prussia was made up of East Prussia, the oldest part, Brandenburg, Pomerania, Upper Silesia and Lower Silesia (usually known as the Province of Silesia). It also included Saxony with Dresden, even Hannover, the Rhein Province and several other counties. In short, Germany consisted of many individual large counties, perhaps states, under the lead of Prussia. And the Mark Brandenburg, my county, was the largest and most densely populated part of Germany. To state that my town was annexed by Hitler is fictitious.

It is also nonsense that Hitler annexed or occupied Kaliningrad, the German Königsberg. East Prussia is (was) one of the oldest German towns, always German until 1945. Towns like Gumbinnen, the famous Allenstein, Trakehnen, even my humble Tharau, they had always been German. No, Hitler did not have to invade us, we Germans were already there.

How big are these areas? Considering the land to the East of the Oder only, take my town as the starting point and go, as the crow flies, to Königsberg, Preußisch Eylau or Gumbinnen in East Prussia, you would cover about the distance from London to Liverpool, you might get your feet wet a bit in the Atlantic; or another way of putting it, start at the Welsh Border and go right across to Great Yarmouth, this time your toes might get wet in the North Sea. If you were to go north–south, say Danzig down to Königgrätz, Silesia, Gleiwitz, Königshütte, and you would cover the distance London–York by the shortest route. You could, just about, pack the whole of England into this area. It was also densely populated.

Hitler did not invade this land, but he did start the war. I don't think for a moment that he was the only maniac who had something to do with it. There will be more to it than meets the eye. As I know my country, people will not have stormed headlong into a war at the drop of a hat. Like my family, they were still trying to recover from the last war. The stew of the Second World War was stirred by more than one cook.

In 1943 Churchill and Stalin agreed that this vast land should be cleared of all Germans and should be given to Poland, thus sanctioning Stalin's invasion of Poland. Was this done to appease Stalin?

If Stalin had wanted to he could have driven his army and tanks right through France to the Atlantic. Who could have stopped him? Was the land deal the alternative to the atomic bomb? A short-term solution? The USA agreed to this inhuman plan and it was made official at the conferences in Potsdam and Yalta in 1945. By the time this plan was finalised the deed had been done, involving 45 million Poles and Germans, to say nothing of the 'displaced' Russians.

What did these leaders think they were doing at a time when anti-German feeling was at its height? It took Hitler several years to murder 6 million innocent Jews and only a few Nazis were hanged for this crime. No one was punished for the crime that was planned and carried out in the East of Germany and Poland. It took the victorious leaders a mere five months between January and May 1945 to murder millions of equally innocent Germans and Poles.

Churchill, Stalin and Roosevelt arranged for the forced expulsion of millions of people from their homeland on a scale that had never happened before. A crime against humanity if ever there was one. Some might say that Churchill, Stalin and Roosevelt resettled Poles and Germans in the West; if so it was just as Hitler 'resettled' Jews in the East.

It was not only Jews that suffered. There were children like me, walking on the road to Soldin, stumbling over bodies and watching as others were turned to a red stain as they collapsed under tanks. A child like me standing on a road to Rhenitz, frozen with terror at the sight of human beings beaten to a pulp. A few weeks later back in the same place burying hundreds of decomposing bodies, among them over 400 teenage boys. There is the heartache over my great-grandfather, beaten and burned alive, the dignified acceptance of her fate of that young mother who had to hand over the body of her dead baby if she wanted to get across the river to save her last child. The dead can hurt you in unexpected ways. The nun. The sound her body made when it hit the floor of the barn with a thud when I cut the rope round her neck. That sound hurts.

The victorious leaders soaked up the admiration and jubilation of their people. Revered by many, reviled by me and millions of others.

If you have any reservations about my sufferings, because as a German I was not equal in status to that of a Jewish child, then you are the kind of monster the world should rightly guard against. You must then also accept that your objections, by necessity, work both ways. You would have to acknowledge that to a Nazi, a Jewish child is not of equal status to a German child. So, the Nazi must be understood and excused as well! Something is very wrong here, isn't it? My mother once said, 'all children like sweets.' Entirely my sentiment.

After 1945 I have also heard and read that the Germans East of the Oder were resettled in the West. But I am not a refugee, not an exile, not an evacuee. I was not resettled. The German language has precisely the right word for what I am — *Vertrieben* — meaning chased out. I was chased out of my home and away from my homeland at gun point. But I lived to tell what happened, while millions of innocents were brutally put to death.

The German people were and are still deeply disturbed about the Hitler years and, like no other nation, share the grief and sufferings inflicted upon the Jewish people. Successive German governments have paid heartfelt and genuine tributes to the horrors which the Jewish people were forced to endure.

But where and when did a German government remember the millions of its own people who like me — the one that got away — bore the brunt of the horror and massacre that engulfed such a huge part of Germany at the hands of the victorious politicians and soldiers? Is it asking too much to have these German dead, equally innocent victims of fascism, remembered? Their sufferings and their deaths must equally serve as a warning, a testimony as to what can happen when international relations break down and intolerance takes over (and money can be made out of weapons). Where is the statue inscribed: 'Sorry, little children'. I miss that statue. Does anyone else?

To change my nationality would be, in my eyes, a betrayal of the innocent dead, not just the ones I buried, whatever their nationality, but of all who suffered this ultimate fate.

I am so thankful that I lived long enough to see the European Union take shape. Some people still have difficulties with the European Union and think of our neighbours as 'foreign'. No, they are not. They are European. To foolishly walk away from this enlightened thinking would plunge Europe back into the tinder box that was 1914. Enlightenment will come, of that I am confident.

And have I become a cynic after all these negative and destructive elements in my life? Definitely not! But a mocking bird, yes. Most frightening for me would have been to become bitter. I am not. That for me would be the final blow dealt to a pitiful being whose life is no longer worth living.

A final word. Children are resilient, aren't they? Then why can I not be in the dark at night? I am always busy at night, writing, reading. Don't wake anyone up, don't make a noise. The light in my room must be switched on. I cannot be in the dark, in case I remember – remember the past. Let there be light. Light and hope for a peaceful future!

INDEX

INDEX